Finding
the
diamond
within

Finding the *diamond* within

10 Ways Every Woman Can *sparkle*

Mary Anderson Stosich

CFI
Springville, Utah

ISBN 13: 978-1-59955-085-5

Published by CFI, an imprint of Cedar Fort, Inc., 2373 W. 700 S., Springville, UT, 84663
Distributed by Cedar Fort, Inc., www.cedarfort.com

LIBRARY OF CONGRESS CATALOGING-IN-PUBLICATION DATA

Stosich, Mary Anderson, 1953-
  Finding the Diamond Within : ten ways every woman can sparkle / Mary Anderson Stosich.
    p. cm.
  ISBN 978-1-59955-085-5
  1. Mormon women—Religious life. I. Title.

BX8641.S84 2007
248.8'430882893—dc22

                              2007032078

Cover design by Nicole Williams
Cover design © 2008 by Lyle Mortimer
Edited and typeset by Lyndsee Simpson Cordes

Printed in the United States of America

10 9 8 7 6 5 4 3 2 1

Printed on acid-free paper

Dedicated to Mama, whose diamond radiates with eternal brilliance.

Table of Contents

✳

Acknowledgments

I wish to express my gratitude to my friends and family who have blessed me with their insights, stories, and suggestions. These include my darling daughters, Lisa Bruneel and Kata Dean; my faithful and true sisters, Estella Crofts and VaLayne Finlayson; one of my precious nieces, DeAnn Edwards; my enduring friend Sharyn Riley; and my beloved husband, Alvin K. Stosich. I also thank past BYU professors who encouraged me to write: Maxine Rowley, Don Norton, and Brenton Yorgason.

The writing of this book began, continued, and ended because of the influence and guidance of Brenton and Margaret Yorgason. They have given me priceless gifts of time, reason, and hope. I will always treasure their sacrifices.

The Diamond in Our Hearts
introduction

*H*ow could she be dying?

She was our three-month-old baby girl. I chose her name, Lisa, when I read it meant "consecrated to God."

But I did not know . . .

Just days before, I had held her to my breast and watched her intently nurse as her tiny fingers clenched around one of my own and held on as if she would never let go. Her miniature fingernails turned white as she squeezed. I softly brushed her wispy, curly hair and counted all ten of her toes.

But this day, the pediatric cardiologist sat across the desk from us. He opened the medical folder that contained Lisa's test results, drew in a deep breath, and looked up with compassionate eyes.

My husband, Al, and I were doing our best to be brave. My tears blurred the pages of diagnosis set before me. Dr. Veasy reached for a note-pad already printed with a simple outline of a perfect heart. He tore off a sheet and began drawing lines, circles, and arrows on the diagram, breaking our own hearts as he showed us the differences between perfect and defective. Between disease and health. Between operable and inoperable . . . between life and death.

Dr. Veasy explained that Lisa had two defects that could possibly be operable if she were able to gain enough strength. The greatest concern was the third, inoperable defect—a devious thief of a life more precious to me than my own. Even if doctors were able to perform the risky surgery,

Lisa's heart would still be unable to sustain normal activity. Fibers had grown through the walls of the left ventricle, making them thick and unable to contract sufficiently to pump blood. Little was known about this rare condition, except for the despairing news that only a handful of affected children had been known to survive to adolescence. As I looked at the notepad with the doctor's alterations, I thought of our baby girl. *Keep holding on, my little darling.*

Al and I were still just kids ourselves—both in our early twenties, and Al barely a college graduate. We were already parents of a robust eighteen-month-old son, AJ. What were we going to do now? What had happened to the happiness and noise of a toddler at my feet and a baby in my arms? What kind of life had just been prescribed on a notepad?

"Will we need to curtail her activity?" I asked, not quite understanding what the doctor had told us. "Will she be able to ride a bike, run and play with other—"

Dr. Veasy softly interrupted, "You will take her home and let her enjoy life in all ways that she is able until . . ."

My husband gave my hand a squeeze. I looked at him. His eyes were brimming with tears of understanding. He had received the message from the doctor that I missed—Lisa's life expectancy was short. There were no comforting answers.

I looked back over my ignorance of the past weeks. It had been a wintry week in Idaho. Lisa had been unable to hold down any food. Her little head would be moist from sweat and her skin pale and white. Her pleadings of tears and whimpering had continued even while we held her. I had taken her to the pediatrician twice already that week, but he had been sure it was only the flu. I had called him again, and this time he impatiently instructed, "Mary, you are just going to have to wait this one out."

We lived in an old farmhouse next to my husband's parents. Al's mother, an affectionate grandmother, shared our deep concern for the baby. She had taught me how to make rice-water for Lisa in hopes that such a mild fluid would stay with her. But then, one night Lisa was in trouble, and we knew it.

Al hauled our mattress from the cold bedroom into the living room. We brought our little ones in next to us and, through the weakening cries of a sick baby, we prayed for wisdom beyond what we deserved. Unconsoled, we tried to sleep. Too young. Too poor. Too naïve.

Trying to sleep was useless, and as though we were responding to a message sent from heaven, we quickly got out of bed and dressed. While Al's parents tended AJ, we raced to the hospital. With little strength left, Lisa could hardly protest the chest x-rays and examination. Her heart and liver were enlarged to several times their normal size. She was in heart failure and needed specialized care not available in Idaho Falls. We rushed to Salt Lake City—three and a half hours away.

We finally arrived at Primary Children's Hospital, where competent, scurrying staff awaited us. In Lisa's failing condition, she could only respond to her fear and pain with a weak grimace. We were allowed to remain by her side.

Holding her little fist in my hand as though I could will her my strength, I prayed with the earnestness of a desperate mother. I could hardly believe that our once-happy, cooing baby now lay almost lifeless under a plastic bubble that delivered oxygen.

Though we spent our nights and days at the hospital, we were hardly alone. My mother and brothers and sisters, who lived within minutes of the hospital, combined with Al's family from Idaho, were supporting us with their time and attentiveness. I lined Lisa's crib with gifts of toys, dressed her in her own clothes, and wrapped her in her own blankets. It was my way of saying, "You still belong to us. Please don't leave."

After days of medication, Lisa's strength miraculously increased. By now we were allowed to pick her up and hold the oxygen to her face. She was doing remarkably well and began to respond with more vigor. The diagnostic testing moved forward. The doctors used a then-new technique—an ultrasound—along with a risky angiogram, but there were no alternatives.

All of this transpired while Al and I anxiously waited with grandparents and family. Lisa made it through another ordeal, and now at last we sat with Dr. Veasy, learning that it was far from over.

My mind once again focused on the doctor and his recommendations. His hope was that the heart medication would allow Lisa the time she needed to gain some strength. Then, hopefully, she would be able to survive open-heart surgery. Repairing her heart's operable defects would add a few years to her life.

Time. When did a day ever mean so much to me? When did a moment with a baby in my arms make me ache so deeply? When did a second of looking into Lisa's eyes ever say so much?

We decided that Al must leave for Idaho Falls to work and care for AJ in the evenings. I took Lisa to my mother's home with the hope that in two weeks she could withstand the intended surgery.

Lisa responded with her inborn personality and determination. Her unconquerable spirit would not be defeated. She began eating again as though she were preparing herself for competition. We returned several times to the doctor during those days for checkups, and she was at last scheduled for repairs to her heart.

I have never believed that God creates a painful experience simply to get our attention. Rather, I believe that life's moments naturally wreak havoc that seems insurmountable. Even so, we have the ability to turn to our Heavenly Father and reach for His help. Oh yes, I pleaded for Lisa's life, but I also prayed that we could accept His will, His plan, and His love.

I was given peace that Lisa was in God's hands, that her life would continue with meaning and purpose. As a mother, this peace and the ensuing trust were my greatest gifts. I was able to focus on her life itself instead of the complexities of it. On the back flap of a small gift book I received at the hospital, I wrote my solemn covenant: "I will make Lisa's dark days light."

Al soon returned with our toddler son. How wonderful my little AJ felt to me! He was lively, healthy, and became my personal, wonderful medicine. We were once again united as a family.

The day of surgery arrived, and the skilled surgeons successfully corrected two of the heart defects. When we saw Lisa again, an incision extended from her chest all the way around to her back. She was attached to life-sustaining machines and needles, and a drainage tube had also been inserted. Blood samples were drawn every few hours, testing for oxygen. Finally, respiratory specialists regularly appeared and gave her dreaded breathing treatments.

Nurses patiently watched as I set up house in the hospital. I spent the nights on the floor under her hospital crib, with only a blanket and pillow. Each move or breath that I could hear meant hope and recovery. When Lisa's cries called for me, I would slide out from under the crib and be there to provide comfort to her.

Days and nights blurred together. Even through all the pain and trauma of recovery, Lisa wanted to live. She fought with a vengeance anything she interpreted as threatening. Her amazing will seemed to give her renewed power and energy. Several times a day, nurses came to perform her regularly scheduled breathing treatments. With total investment, Lisa screamed through each one. I could barely remain in the room, but neither could I bear to leave. A baby only a few months old, somehow knowing the miracle of life, decided to fight for the right to live it.

Through bad days and better days, Lisa continued to heal. To the surprise of everyone, she made it home for Christmas! I was armed with prescriptions that she would supposedly need her entire life.

Lisa's recovery was startling and magnificent. She grew and flourished like every other child, often with a fierce intensity. After one year, her medication was discontinued. After two years, the cardiologists released her from routine care. They found no existing evidence of heart disease, except a slight murmur that gave no cause for alarm.

As our family life normalized, Lisa lived with full force. She missed nothing. She rode a bike and ran and played with other children. Then she became a star athlete in high school. She received athletic and academic scholarships to college, and now—years later—she is married and a mother herself, experiencing the joy she gave me.

Over the years, I have asked myself: What was it about that little soul? What was the real condition of her heart—her emotional heart? What was it that gave her such determination? What did she—an infant—know that helped her through the pain and hardships of such invasive surgery and the complications of heart disease?

Could each of our hearts have a condition that goes far beyond our auricles and ventricles? Were we born with a heart that beats with an incredible desire to live? Could it be that within each of us is a condition of worthwhile cause? Is there something deep inside that allows us to search for purpose, for an opportunity to find joy?

I believe that the Light of Christ, which "giveth light to all things," has enriched every cell of our hearts with wonder and with the importance of life. As I have looked into Lisa's eyes, I have thought that it must be more than anxiety. Perhaps she just couldn't bear to miss a moment.

Hearts and Diamonds

A heart is more than a muscle beating lifeblood through veins. It's quite like a diamond: our memories and feelings are pressed with emotion into its every cell, crystallizing experience into potential beauty. Our experiences are related to our purpose. They beg for our courageous embrace, not our withdrawal. This precarious mortality brings our hearts to gratitude even though sometimes it seems to oppose our happiness. We look for another day, another chance. And then, in our becoming—our precious crystallizing—we finally know that happiness will not cower in a corner.

Precious living contrasts with the easy life. It endures the pressure that a diamond requires. And after endurance, such living still asks for the Master Craftsman to cut and polish. This master is not new to our lives. There is no need to wonder, *Is He capable?* He knows our hearts. He knows our history, because from the beginning He has been there with and for us. He has the knowledge and pure love to precisely cut each facet in a particular way, exposing our own particular beauty and infinite worth.

The casket lid was closed on a young woman's life that had been cut short by ovarian cancer. It had been an ordinary life by most people's standards. No great inventions, no wordy books, no moments of fame on TV, no medals won. Yet, the words of love and the expressions of gratitude testified of the beautiful life that a precious, ordinary woman could live in just thirty-nine years.

In anguish, her husband whispered, through his tears, all he knew of Heaven's cruel design. Could anything console their six, motherless children? Their mother had loved and cared for them. But life, as they had known it, would never be the same. They would no more see her smile, hear her voice, or feel the caress of her fingertips.

The pallbearers—each one a close girlfriend—were decisively brave. Still with streaming tears, they kept a promise made in happier times as they gripped the casket's handles. It made sense. The women had loved, laughed, and cried together for years, and this day, while hymns rolled from the organ, they would bear their friend down the chapel aisle.

What had looked ordinary to everyone else had become infinitely precious to those who had lived within the reach of her love.

We Are Diamonds

There are times when questions relentlessly beg for answers. We ask, "Do I matter? What is my worth in this huge world? What should I give my life for? If I were gone, would I be missed?"

We discover happiness when we stop trying to copy another person. Happiness beckons when we start living a life that is strengthened by our faith in Jesus Christ.

My friend Sandy lost her diamond ring in a lake. Tearful searches ended, and the hot summer weeks drifted by. Sandy never got used to the bare spot on her ring finger. It wasn't the price tag of the gem. It was the meaning and what it helped her remember—years of life, trials, and love. She never lost hope of finding it.

In early autumn, Sandy and her husband launched their boat one more time. With high anticipation, they motored across the lake to the spot. By now, the receding water had left behind a beach of mud, where they would hopefully find Sandy's ring. Armed with metal detectors, Sandy and her husband jumped out of their beached boat.

They staked out a grid and began a careful, calculated search. They hoped and prayed that the detectors would sound off the news of a lost and cherished ring. As they sunk knee-deep in thick mud, so did their hearts. Was this impossible? It seemed futile.

After only twenty minutes, the detector alarmed them to an object. Screaming, hoping, and praying, Sandy dug and squished into the mud, and her hand squeezed around a small object! She opened her fist to reveal a lump of mud. She rubbed it a little, and a facet of her lost diamond ring caught the light. She put it on, a perfect fit! Screaming in delight, she ran to a little stream close by, swished it around in the water, and there it was on her finger—her once lost, now found, gleaming ring!

Somehow, out there in the sunshine of a blessed day, Sandy's diamond seemed even more beautiful than before! Perhaps it was because of the added value of tears, longing, waiting, hoping, and searching. Rescued and treasured once more, its rediscovery gave it even greater value.

※

Perhaps we have overlooked our worth and happiness. Maybe we are lost in deep water or are wandering fruitlessly, begging for the world to acknowledge our worth. Perhaps our shine is dimmed and covered with mud, and maybe we are blind to our meaning and purpose because we think of ourselves as of little worth.

Thankfully, we are never lost from our Creator. By living true to the heart He gave us, we will experience the polishing needed to reveal the facets of our diamond. It is the treasure that can be found in every woman's heart.

10 Ways Every Woman Can *sparkle*

chapter 1

Build a Fortress of Femininity
protecting happiness by nurturing

We rented our new house sight unseen. We had found out about it from someone who knew someone who knew someone else who knew us. I knew we were crazy. After a long day of caravanning hundreds of miles behind a U-Haul moving van, we pulled into our new cul-de-sac. At that time we had four children, a picture-perfect family—at least in photographs where they were all frozen in smiling poses.

As we pulled to a stop, I thought about our babies who were elementary school age. I realized that we had nothing over on them. We were in this together. What was this insane decision Al and I had made to move hundreds of miles away from all we loved and knew, just to put bread on the table? Panic and excitement zinged every nerve in my body—I was just about to see what we would call home.

When we pulled in front of the house, I insisted that we double-check the address. I thought for sure there had been a mistake. How could this be? There stood a beautiful two-story home, hugged by evergreens and roses in full bloom, with a parched-white sidewalk leading to the front door. A moment later, I closed my eyes, hoping with all my heart that the key would actually unlock the door to our new life. Click. The door opened and, as if a dam had broken, our children flooded through the entryway. Al and I almost crept inside—wondering if we were going to be arrested. We looked at each other in amazement.

A charming brick fireplace graced the dining room, and a sunken living room cheerfully revealed the roses outside through large windows. A spacious kitchen—complete with a large pantry, a view of the backyard, and a sliding door—led conveniently to the laundry and den. A vaulted ceiling and gracious stairway ascended to encircle the entire main floor with a balcony. Spacious bedrooms, a sewing room, and TV nook awaited our invasion.

The good news continued. As we walked out the sliding door, we stepped onto a stone patio embedded among luscious lawn, shrubs, shade trees, and fruit trees. Grapevines arched over an arbor that formed an entry to a vegetable garden. My voice—something between singing and praying—kept repeating, "I can't believe this. I can't believe this!"

Our moving van was soon unloaded, and we were home. It was a feeling so delicious I could scarcely take it in.

The problem came after days of no ringing phones, no knocks on the door, and no neighbor children running in and out. The truth is, a beautiful home couldn't replace the beautiful people we had left behind. Homesickness quietly seeped in as a contagious infection of loneliness and yearning.

It was Jane Austen who said, "Every neighborhood should have a great lady."[1] I was just about to meet ours. That moment I will never forget—a knock at our very own front door! I literally raced the kids to be the one to open it. There on our front doorstep stood Julie Engstrom—a petite, five-foot, smiling angel of mercy with a mission. She and her husband, Jerry, had three daughters and lived less than a block away. When she heard that we had moved in, she made a list of everyone the children would want to meet, then took us on a walk to introduce us to our neighbors.

Julie nurtured us with her interest. She learned of our hobbies and discovered what made each of us tick. She did not operate from the facade of a welcome wagon but from a caring heart. Her connection was instant, sincere, and constant. She didn't give a briefing; she offered friendship. Because of her care, our two families developed a love and trust that has lasted a lifetime.

Julie not only nurtured her own kids and ours but children throughout the community. While hers were young, she operated a preschool in her home and gained the trust of hundreds of parents. After her children were grown, she returned to public school teaching, but she didn't leave preschool quietly. She encouraged me to take over her preschool business by hauling box-loads of supplies to my home. She simply gave them to me with no stipulations or expectations, then encouraged parents to enroll in my program.

Julie continued her education career, developing a program for children with reading difficulties that was adopted by several schools. She became noted for her talents and was respected among her colleagues. But Julie didn't stop there. Her nurturing strengthened the women of her church, whom she would visit after school hours. She took them meals and organized service projects, then gave extra time to those who were sick or in need.

I watched Julie for years as her powerful influence affected the lives of countless individuals. Former students would ask her to write references for job and college applications, and because she had invested time in appreciating their unique traits, her letters of recommendation witnessed the life of another.

Loving and caring never weakened Julie. Instead, she dug in her heels with strong opinions because of the sureness found only beyond herself.

Julie recently moved on in her career to teaching at the university level, but the important things have not changed. She holds the adoration of hundreds of people. Her strength, power, and brains have not elicited fear or intimidation. Instead, she is revered and counted as a friend and mentor. She is loved and appreciated because of how people feel about themselves when they are around her.

Nurturing—The Fortress of Protection

Not too many years ago, our society made it difficult to discuss certain topics. These "unmentionables" were terms born of crime, hate, and immorality. If conversations did take place, they were discreet and most often considered ugly or embarrassing. Great care was taken not to injure innocence. Now, only a few years later, we read about them, talk about them, and engross ourselves in them. We find entertainment in the blatant and lewd and have almost eliminated the list of unmentionables. In their place, the new unmentionables seem to be terms born of morality, love, and decency. The list includes the words *pure love* and *self-sacrifice*.

It is from these unmentionable acts of nurturing that great timbers are hewn for a mighty fortress of protection. With every act of nurturing, we build this fortress with thick, tall timbers—well-placed and buttressed. Without this fortress, we remain vulnerable to deadly germ warfare—infectious self-absorption. It sprawls its invading fibers that twist around our hearts and strangle our natural ability to build relationships. These fibers thread through our brains, interrupting intelligent thoughts and sincere communication. They coil round and round into a heavy ball of fear in our stomachs because we can never look, speak, or act perfectly enough. Self-absorption saps our energy and leaves us with little power to live our lives. Rather than reaching out to others, we devour ourselves in selfish labor. We are unwittingly left feeling like empty, powerless shells and experience painful self-cannibalism.

I have my nerve, but I must admit that several times I have almost lost it while writing this chapter. In this world of searching for self-fulfillment, who dares to say that nurturing is a powerful gender role that protects us? As I write, I worry, "Will women misunderstand nurturing to mean confinement, fewer opportunities, or silenced opinions?" Many of us have twisted the truth into a knot of misunderstanding, ignorantly thinking that caring will foster weakness and that taking the time to love will set us behind.

There are those who vengefully fight against the truth that joy comes from nurturing others. Perhaps it is their fear that beats the war drum in their chests—a fear that their lives will be swallowed up in some sort of sorry insignificance. Remaining in their own tiny bed of debilitating self-absorption, they suffer untold loneliness and frustration. They may never realize that their growth and healing are found as they comprehend and satisfy the needs of others as well as their own.

Calling a Truce

Can we just talk? Let's call a truce to the war that's been going on between us—women of directions. Not direction—*directions*. The unapproachable task of naming all of our directions is comparable to naming the numberless ways that we as women may find to nurture and mother.

In a very real sense, nurturing is not dependent on giving birth. There are opportunities all around you where people need your particular "mothering." They can be found in your immediate and extended families, your friendships, your professions, and in every single person you meet.

There is no "one life fits all." There are women who stay at home with children and husbands. There are women without children and women without husbands. There are career women who juggle and twist. There are single mothers who muster a brave fight against the odds. From seemingly ordinary to outlandish, each—with extremely hard work, talent, and vision—will have the opportunity to nurture and love all whom they can reach. What we all must learn is that happiness does not come by venting disappointment, resentment, or anger but by expressing love. It is time to honor the good and beauty in each other. Aha! We must nurture each other!

Don't Recycle It. Trash It.

Although I refer to nurturing as crucial gender role, I am fully aware that it is not, nor should it be, peculiar to only women. Certainly men nurture and love. It is a skill that more women are asking for and more men are learning. Thank goodness! But women seem to be born with an innate capacity and yearning. Recent research gives evidence that females actually are born with sensitivity, tenderness, and concern, and that they have inborn desires to nurture and love.[2] You can be sure that ignoring these qualities and downplaying their importance will result in want and emptiness.

The extreme sweep of the radical feminist pendulum has tried to bully down not only traditions that strengthen our homes and relationships but also the very endowments of nature. When I realized this, I was caught off guard. It was in the 1970s, and I remember the excitement I felt. Equal rights for women! Fairness and respect!

Now, however, it seems that it's really not about equal rights. It is about giving up what is dear and important. Does equality really mean that I must be apologetic for being true to my feminine heart? What if I love being a mother? What if I want to raise my own children? What if I enjoy being married and making the necessary commitments and sacrifices?

My life was littered with claims that I was wasting my intelligence and creativity because I had a family instead of a career! It was garbage that demeaned my basic need to nurture.

This garbage continues to be recycled, like old cardboard, showing up in our lives with:

- Our wants are the only ones that matter.
- Equality is a matter of sameness, not of importance and value.
- Commitment to a relationship is not only boring, it is stifling!
- Children don't need parents, only quality day care.
- Men don't have feelings, and their needs are a nuisance to us as women.
- Gender differences are negligible and should be ignored or disregarded.

These ideas continue to harass us. It's time for us to take out the garbage and start our lives anew. The following truths are refreshing; we must cherish them like an heirloom so that we can pass them on to future generations:

- We nurture others with positive influence.
- We care about others and ourselves because we are all in this together.
- We talk, cry, laugh, and love together.
- We look on others with compassion and admiration.
- We need the help and influence of good men, priesthood leaders, and our husbands, and they need us.
- We look forward with hope while we develop patience.
- We teach something to everyone we encounter.
- We give our time, and we smile as we help.

Several summers ago my girlfriends and I decided to take our children to a nearby hotel for an overnight mini-vacation. It was a Holiday Inn that had all kinds of games and a huge swimming pool. The kids were thrilled, and within moments of our arrival they were going wild in the pool. Later that evening we mothers slithered down into the hot tub to relax while our children continued to play.

Soon we were joined by a woman who had come to town on business. She had retreated to the hot tub to relax and was probably horrified at the sight of several children trotting back and forth from pool to hot tub. We started to chat, and she asked me what I did. I smiled and wondered if the five bodies weren't enough for an answer, but I replied that I was a stay-at-home mother.

"How confining!" she responded. "I couldn't bear the boredom. Don't you wonder what you're missing?"

This was not a new question to me. Moments of evaluation had become defining, and I knew that my life was rich and meaningful. I had a husband who supported our family; we had children, a home, and great friends. My world was small but never boring.

Further, I had gained confidence from skills I had learned as a mother. I had increased my talents while teaching my children, and I had widened the boundaries of my life with wonderful people outside my home.

While this woman knew of her own life, she could not imagine the breadth of nurturing. I was not "missing" anything. Nurturing had become a fortress that helped protect me from infectious self-absorption, and while raising a family I was also gaining experience and developing personal character, strength, and competence.

Motherhood has a refining power. It offers difficult choices that expose our true selves. Do we decide to build our fortress of femininity and enlarge our borders by loving and appreciating our children? Or do we dread this responsibility and wish it away?

On the one hand, as women, we need extra courage to face pregnancy, gain weight, and hang over the toilet. We need courage as we helplessly watch varicose veins stream up and down our legs. On the other hand, having a baby has become another popular fad where we have a little darling to dress only in name-brand clothes. We then add all the modern equipment, toys, and educational opportunities the world has to offer. It is a world in which the infinite worth of our baby may be obscured by a glitzy parade.

Mothering requires courageous women who will look at childbearing with expectations of sacrifice that go around the bend, where we can't see into our own future. It requires women who will find joy even from children who have a way of breaking apart our best-laid plans. Motherhood is a most unglamorous decision but one of infinite worth.

Mothering involves the ridiculous risk of unmet expectations, heartache, loneliness, ingratitude, loss, and sorrow. What kind of woman invests time, talents, and everything she has into someone completely needy, incapable, immature, and sometimes downright selfish? Still, there are those of us eager to sign up. And the return? The final figures can't tell the entire story—all the black and red might look like bankruptcy! But if we could unfold all the truths that wrap around and through the bottom line, I am sure our ledger would say something like, "Being a mother was well worth every minute."

As we approach the many skills involved in nurturing, we are comforted by our prophets and modern-day revelation. They assure us of our abilities and responsibilities through "A Proclamation to the World," which states that mothers are primarily responsible for the nurture of their children.

Whether we are mothers or not, the contrast between nurturing and selfishness remains. Consider the smell of selfishness compared to the fragrance of nurturing.

Nurturing	**Selfishness**
Looks to others' needs	Has only self-centered concerns
Wants to heal and nourish	Will wound for gain
Gives and receives love	Cares more for pleasure or seduction
Desires to teach or elevate	Criticizes others
Cheers	Ignores

We would each be wise to contemplate our own attitudes. We must understand that we are at risk from the toxicity of the world's recycled garbage that can continue to poison our lives.

Self-Transformation

Transformations not only happen to those we nurture but also to ourselves. Change comes through the act of self-sacrifice, which is as enriching for the giver as it is for the receiver. We give our best to others but, surprisingly, before the tallies are made, our best has been given back to us, and we stand magnified. It feels good because we were neither robbed nor used; we freely offered a portion of ourselves. We might have thought our sacrifice would leave an emptiness, but instead it brought an incredible fullness.

Love deepens as we accommodate new understanding, and resiliency increases because our increasing wisdom takes no offense. We actually change into a person with more influence, depth, and territory. We nurture not with puny apron strings attached but with powerful bungee cords of love. These binding cords endure stretching and connect us intimately to those we love.

The Unending Influence of Nurturing

Growing up in a home managed by a single mother had unique challenges. Mother was the queen and ruler. Livestock, gardening, irrigating, paying the bills, managing money, buying, selling, and building, as well as cleaning, cooking, sewing, and raising children were all in her realm of womanhood. I was steeped in the simmering pot of Mother's own version of the Women's Movement long before it was in the newspapers or magazines. Mom's style was liberating in that I was exposed to experiences my friends had no taste of. My experiences were in sharp contrast to the ideas that were emerging on the cultural horizon.

Mother was before her time in her ideas of what a woman could accomplish. She was also enriched with the wisdom that nurturing was enlivening. Though she led our household with tenacity and focus, she encircled her strength and will with softness and beauty. She refused to denounce the value of love and service. She lived without apology for loving her children more than prestige and with no regret for giving her very best to others in need.

One of my richest experiences began when I started as a seven-year-old piano student. Piano lessons were not a "do-it-yourself" experience. I was watched over even when I didn't want or deserve it.

My love for music began at one of the routine get-togethers at our home that mother hosted for teenagers. One of these young people, Maryanne Nunley, could play the piano, and it was on this night that Mother asked her to give me piano lessons.

Looking back, I know Mom wanted to give Maryanne the chance to teach almost as much as she wanted to give me the opportunity to learn. She could see the benefit for both.

At first, Maryanne profusely declined. She claimed that her lack of training proved her unqualified. But Mom didn't back down. Out of love and respect for her, Maryanne agreed. As I stood watching on, the deal was confirmed with a warm embrace.

Mother, Maryanne, and other teachers nurtured me and taught me the value of giving as I learned to play the piano. I visited rest homes with my mother. There I played for my aged friends. Then I began teaching lessons to other children in the neighborhood. Through these opportunities of service, I received the warmth and fulfillment of nurturing.

That was many years ago. Recently I walked into a funeral home to pay tribute to my first piano teacher. Maryanne had never married, but her life had been full of music. Even more important, it was filled with nurturing. She had spent years teaching piano, giving of her talents and enlarging her sphere of influence along the way. I thought of Mother nurturing Maryanne, Maryanne nurturing me, and then me nurturing others—all through the magical realm of music. I thought of the expanded influence of Maryanne as she exhibited a life of fulfillment, protected by her fortress of femininity. Now part of Maryanne, Mother, and myself lives in others. Who knows how far the impact that began in front of my family's old piano will ripple out?

Relief Comes from Nurturing

Throughout my teenage years, my oldest sister and her family lived within walking distance of our home. I loved my nieces and nephew dearly and many times would gladly baby-sit. It was in my sister's home that I learned the luscious feelings of feeding a baby and the proud accomplishment of bathing three kids together. I remember counting to one thousand while I patted a crying baby on the back and then crawling out of the room and hurrying about to clean the house before my sister returned. These experiences melted my heart and refined my inner-self. They brought me relief from teenage worries and helped me see that there was more to life than high school drama.

Nurturing experiences will bring us relief from a too-small world. A note on a coworkers desk, a compliment, a visit to the lonely. There are endless lists of kindness, and there's an endless supply of joy. Nurturing will not only bring us true fulfillment but will also offer sanctuary to all who feel of our love.

You Can Be a Heroine

Examples of nurturing may not seem as romantic as a heroine standing on a hill with the wind of victory blowing through her hair. I always wanted to look like that! Somehow, however, I was the woman who stood on the driveway and yelled, "Come home for dinner!"

A heroine you will be—with eyes that search and discover the true surprise with ears that hear needs and pleadings, with a mouth that smiles and knows how to laugh, with shoulders straightened by courage and conviction, with hands callused from effort. Heroines have hearts that have been broken yet left unscarred and willing feet that will most certainly take the next step.

A popular notion is to be tough and thoughtless. It is easy to think that if we are tender and feel too much, we might lose our place in line or get shoved out. We may foolishly believe that less caring will get us more equality.

My mother, Julie, Maryanne, and countless other heroic women illuminate a well-kept secret: giving to others what they need is not weakness. Selfless love protects our beauty, strength, and happiness. It doesn't take money or possessions; it requires progress toward self-mastery and devotion to a greater cause than self.

Nurturers do not fight for fame. Instead, they have followers of their love and strength. Their only captives are those of adoration.

From our experiences of giving a real part of ourselves, we enjoy the protection of our fortress of femininity. As we respond to our Savior's command to follow him, we begin to realize how this exquisite facet brings fulfillment and joy into every corner of our soul.

Notes

1. Cathryn Michon and Pam Norris, *Jane Austen's Little Advice Book* (New York: HarperCollins, 1996), 7.
2. Steven E. Rhoads, *Taking Sex Difference Seriously* (San Francisco: Encounter Books, 2004), 18–19.

chapter 2

Discover the Truth
revealing superwoman

Let's begin with a confession. I have never had it all together, except perhaps once for five minutes just as I started having labor pains. I sat staring at the teensy undershirts and cloth diapers I had purchased for my first baby. I was in what I think you could call the Twilight Zone—the only time in my life I remember my work being finished. It was a moment of peaceful ignorance of what lay ahead and what was slipping into my past, where nothing ruled except the very second at hand, and that was about how long it lasted.

This was the same day that I quit my job. I had it all together because I had left my classroom with perfect, detailed instructions and lesson plans for the remainder of the year. With a huge lump of good-bye in my throat and an ache in my heart, I had hugged every preschool child. I had picked up my last huge paycheck and was ready to become a mother.

My house was completely clean—all three rooms. Dinner was over and dishes were washed—all two cups, plates, and forks, as well as the pan from the green bean casserole. There was a small supply of food in our cupboard, and a gallon of milk, two squares of margarine, and a small square of Velveeta cheese sat neatly in the refrigerator.

It was obvious that I had it all together. The laundry basket was empty, the car had a little gas, and Al and I had even planted a little garden in a narrow plot of dirt in the backyard of our rented basement apartment. If that wasn't enough, my toenails were polished! Heaven knows that there was no way I was going into the delivery room for our

21

first baby and hoisting my feet up into the stirrups with ugly toenails.

Another reason I had it all together? I had no other choice—my mother-in-law was coming!

Thirty years and five children later, having it all together is merely a hilariously funny phrase. Deep inside, I know it is simply never going to happen. Every day there are myriad things left undone, partly damaged spaces where edifying words should have been spoken, and the feeling of forgetting something I should have remembered.

False Templates

In a previous century, women were not usually allowed to gain a formal education. Some scientists actually thought their brains might explode. These women were given a life template lacking in individuality and truth. In an actual experiment, a woman was isolated and monitored while she was fed information and ideas. A profound discovery—her brain didn't explode! It took extreme courage by a few men to instigate the cultural acceptance that educating females would not be a waste.

Even though we have come a long way, we are still bombarded with false templates. We keep trying to fit into something too tight or too large in all the wrong places. It is a template most of us didn't even ask for, but we are supposed to plug our lives into it and call it success.

While fitting into the modern template, we are expected to be all and do all. We are even driven to postpone or even discard dreams of motherhood—the unthinkable sacrifice for "better things to do." Maybe give birth, but only if we have a perfectly furnished house, a nice car, and beautiful clothes. Positively, someone else should raise our babies, and keep in mind that we really don't need a man around to father. We could do that too!

Recognition is being ripped away from women who know their souls, who love their femininity. It is being torn from those who would dare choose to mother, as though mothering holds no value.

And so, many women who yearn for acceptance and accomplishment are arrested in their missions of love. They are squeezed into templates of "acceptable behavior" that have demeaned the value of a sacred chamber of their dreams.

Impostors

In the sixties, in a new game show, a panel of three or four people would claim to be a certain person. A contestant would question the panel members to decide between the "real" person and the impostors. Sometimes an impostor could completely fool the contestants and be chosen as the winner. I loved watching the game and picking the "real" person. I was often shocked when the host would say, "Would the real 'so and so' please stand up?" I couldn't believe it when an impostor had fooled me.

Now, we are not in a game show, but clever impostors often fool us. As we search for direction, meaning, and validation in our lives, we are often answered with lies, empty promises, and attacks. We have been led along as though we were mindless. We have been programmed as though we were heartless, and we have been shamed in our goodness. Impostors may pose as superwomen but are only fragments of reality. They often come from tiny self-contained worlds where lack of love both putrefies and petrifies.

I am reminded of these scriptures in 2 Timothy 3:1–7, which clearly define invading imposters:

> This know also, that in the last days perilous times shall come.
> For men shall be lovers of their own selves, covetous, boasters, proud, blasphemers, disobedient to parents, unthankful, unholy,
> Without natural affection, trucebreakers, false accusers, incontinent, fierce, despisers of those that are good,
> Traitors, heady, highminded, lovers of pleasures more than lovers of God;
> Having a form of godliness, but denying the power thereof: from such turn away.
> For of this sort are they which creep into houses, and lead captive silly women laden with sins, led away with divers lusts,
> Ever learning, and never able to come to the knowledge of the truth.

The term *superwoman* is extremely defined! There are many variations, but a visible example would be the ageless female. She must have a gorgeous body and trendy hair and be witty and intelligent. She must have the ability to forecast the future in order to make perfect decisions. She could be a great cook but would never be subservient in the kitchen. She maintains a perfect home. If married, her man likely adores every move she makes, but she can put him aside whenever necessary and even acquire a new one. If she has children, they never get in her way or slow her down. And she almost always makes money—lots of it.

That definition is quite the costume, and I have seen it hanging in many closets, all glamorous, smooth, and velvety. But I wonder how it would ever fit me. It looks too tight in all the wrong places and too big in all the others. It makes me wonder, "What is wrong with me?"

Impostors, though varied, are always empty on the inside. Let me name a few. Let's start with the supermother who drives twenty carpools, always looks twenty-five years old, speaks three languages at home, serves as the Relief Society president, has written a recipe book containing her original gourmet menus, and is interviewed on the *Today Show* about her successful parenting style.

Another impostor sports the importance of individualism, a new car, new jewelry, new clothes, and a new husband. Hers is a life where self-pleasure runs the clock but will never be able to turn back the hands of missed opportunities.

There is also the impostor of the idealized working mother who can have everything at once and sacrifice nothing. It is a false image of a smiling, carefree woman with kids peacefully at day care.

It is time to reveal true superwomen—not imposters, but women in their average, everyday spheres of influence.

The real superwoman is the young mother with the baby-blues still trying to breast-feed, the housewife with "bed head" cheerfully waking the household, the jogger with a doublewide stroller, the night-school student with diapers and binkies in her backpack. She is the mother searching at the deep end of life's pool, where she saw her child fall. Her face could be framed with locks of silken, white hair and lined and trenched with wrinkles from smiles and pain.

We spot another superwoman as the still-single career woman contributing in her work as she finds fulfillment and changes even a small but important part of the world. In careers too numerous to name, she works for a need and a cause. She is a woman who demonstrates character and influence. She prays for her man to come along, but she doesn't sit by the front door, pining. She works while some hopes come alive and others quietly die. The world expects this woman's independence even when she's down. She is always the one to get the grocery cart after someone else's baby sat drooling in it with a lollipop. But her career mind may also treasure dreams that she can't bear to speak out loud anymore. They are dreams of a husband, faithful love, and little eyes looking upward. She also considers the fear and pressure of what she would give up if she ever found that dream. She may be the target of poisoned questions such as the famous "Are you dating anyone yet?" Such a woman survives the weekend and welcomes Monday morning.

A superwoman is often a working mother who must face the tough decisions of what to keep for the heart's sake and what to throw out for work's sake. Should she feel tenderness, panic, or frustration when she sees her home phone number, for the umpteenth time, on her caller ID? Certainly the impostor is not the mother leaning up against the shut door of the day care, tears streaming down her face as she listens to her toddler finish crying, "Mama."

A magazine would never picture the bravely buried tears of a single mother's loneliness. It might exclude the beautiful scene of a mom curled up on the bed beside her child, her eyelids held open by angels as she listens to the events of recess, ball practice, or prom night.

Where is this woman? She can be seen in many places. There is no mold of shoulds but a symphony of differences and ideas. The only absolute is her loving touch, which shapes the world by shaping singular lives.

Difficulties are there for each of us, regardless of our role. Our secrets are mostly well kept—as least we think they are. As private and as deep as they are, they give us unique personalities, wealthy minds, and sensitive spirits.

The Real Superwoman

So I ask, "Will the real superwoman please stand up?" I know that not many believe they could answer to this title. But let's change the definition. Female—any age. Beautiful in her individuality. Humble in her success. Still alive and kicking, even in her mistakes. Helpful. Loving. Concerned. Sometimes confident, and sometimes hammered and hidden. Eager in her questions, and on the verge of change.

As Latter-day Saint women, we are taught not to compare ourselves to others or to be imposters. Even so, somehow the ugly belief that we should be just like everyone else over-runs us. Our self-inflicted wreckage incapacitates us. We resign ourselves to live only slightly and then die devastating deaths of mistaken identity . . . hoping all the while that we will inherit the celestial kingdom.

All this long while, we don't realize that our differences are simple and small—but of grand importance. And all this long while, we don't realize that our similarities are great and complex—and also of grand importance—because they hold us together in the same family of God. We struggle against the truths that we are all both great and small, and that we are all both special and ordinary. These truths are the reasons that we must give, love, and receive from each other—all part of filling the measure of our creation.

Freedom from the Torture of Comparison

Does your soul weep from a constant flogging of comparison? Each lash of the whip tears you down and apart. Drop the whip.

For each of us, this provides a sacred moment to pause and decide to be true to our own beauty. We can let go of all the envy, the competition, and the striving. Why compare ourselves to someone who is not even cut out to be us? We must bury the whip.

In our dependable handbook for life, the Book of Mormon, we read the account of the Lamanites who buried their destructive, murderous weapons of war for peace—because of their love for others. As Latter-day Saint sisters, we must bury our weapons of comparison. We should allow our "selves" to live with the joyful freedom of being individuals, then extend that same gift to others.

One night, I tucked my ten-year-old daughter in bed. Sitting in my usual spot at her side, then looking down at the beautiful creature that God had placed in my trust, I witnessed misery spilling out from the trembling corners of her lips. She wanted to speak, yet dared not. Huge tears rolled down her temples into her dark hair.

"My darling! What is the matter?"

True to female nature, she replied, "Nothing, Mom."

We all know that when there are tears, the word *nothing* means "something." I opened my heart to her simple, candid, heartbreaking explanation.

"I want to be like Lisa," she continued; then more tears came as she wept on my shoulder.

This was our Kata. She was so full of fun and joy that the room lit up before she entered—as though it were announcing her arrival. She sang and danced while she set the table. When life became too serious, we were entertained with her drama and humor. She was also as gentle as moonlight and twinkling stars.

Horrified that I had not been the perfect mother who would have been able to instill in Kata that her individuality was of incredible value, I did what imperfect mothers do. I cried back, hugged, rocked, and then whispered again and again, "I love *you*."

That night's drama produced no immediate results. As with Kata, the acceptance of who we are usually doesn't come like a tidal wave that washes all the waste out to sea. Rather, it comes more like a sprinkling, drop by drop, until one day the miracle appears.

The miracle of solid self-esteem does not come by mere chance, but rather by honestly answering difficult questions and working toward goals. Like Kata, this is how we are able to grow into women of poise, charity, and charm.

Our habit of making invalid personal assessments when we are children produces an unnecessary, extended list of failures, though, with close examination, those failures become our miracles. They represent the copycats we could never be. They allow us the excitement of expressing our own possibility.

A friend of mine, Paula, told me of an event she attended where "Miss Somebody" was speaking. "Miss Somebody" spoke on how to plan out our lives, how to get organized, how to look beautiful, and so forth. Paula said that "Miss Somebody" was exquisitely beautiful. She had the figure, the hair, the face, and the personality.

After the event, instead of being inspired, Paula came away with an extra portion of self-loathing. She drove home alone—crying the entire way. She thought, *I will never be like her. I am so inadequate.* Paula even forgot that she had lost a hundred pounds that year and had maintained her weight for seven months! She could not look at her own experience and appreciate her own improvements. She truly couldn't feel appreciation or respect for "Miss Somebody" because she was filled with envy.

Since that evening, Paula has been trying to catch herself when she begins comparative thinking. Recently, her understanding deepened as she explained to one of her married friends that she was overcoming the habit of envying married women. She decided she must find fulfillment as a single woman, thinking perhaps she would never marry.

Paula's friend quietly replied, "Well, I am married, but I am still empty because I can't have a baby. All I do is look at married women who are pregnant and wish to be them."

Paula told me something I will never forget: "Ultimately, we must live with ourselves and love ourselves."

It is impossible for the comparing to end as long we live envious lives. My mother once told me, "There will always be someone smarter, someone more beautiful, and someone more talented. Just love yourself, Mary, and be thankful for everyone."

Love and Appreciate Yourself

Each of us is one out of six billion. There is no duplicate, no mold. Loving and appreciating who we are does not mean that suddenly we are supposed to think that no one is better looking than we are, that no one has a talent superior to ours, or that we are perfect. It means that we feel peaceful gratitude for our body, our mind, and our virtues. It means opening our heart to God's love for us. It is understanding and admitting that we really are someone precious in the sight of Heavenly Father.

Loving and appreciating ourselves allows us to enjoy the talents of someone else because we can admire their richness without belittling ourselves. Though it means living without envy, it nevertheless embraces the desire to become better. It is the discarding of old, jealous wishes. It includes raising a goal, like a brilliant banner, to the top of our own pole of perfection.

Lies versus Truth

Not long ago, I was talking with a young woman who was an amazing athlete oozing with talent. She was a lean 5'10" and had long, brown hair that swung down her back, beautiful brown eyes, and a great brain. To look at her, one would think that she had everything. To the contrary, she worried about her unusual height and lacked self-confidence when not participating in a sport.

After we discussed some of this young woman's harsh experiences— similar to those most of us had while growing up—I suggested to her that it was time for her to rid herself of all the negatives she was tightly holding. Doing so would allow her to embrace the beautiful truths about herself. I asked if she would apologize to herself for closing her heart to God's love. I advised her to try to see her beauty and worth as God saw her.

I spoke fervently. "Every time you say something negative, say right out loud, 'Cancel that!' Then every day say things to yourself such as, 'I am lovely. I walk with my chin up and smile. I am grateful for my body. I am beautiful. I am smart. I have talents. I love my uniqueness. I can change any habit I want. I am a thinker. I am strong and courageous.' "

This lovely young woman, who had everything going for her except her attitude, looked up with sincere and wondering eyes and asked, "Mary, don't you think I would just be lying to myself?"

I silently considered my reply. "Lying to yourself? Telling yourself that you are worthy, that you have talents, that you have your own distinct beauty and natural gifts—this is lying? Is it lying to admit you are a divine creation? Believing and saying that you are wonderful—that is a lie?"

Telling yourself of your fantastic potential and worth, that you are able and have strength to overcome, that you have something to contribute to others! These are lies? Telling yourself that you can look people in the eye because you are full of love is a lie? These are not lies; they are even more than possibilities. They describe the crystal in the diamond.

Lies battle to defeat our divine nature. They discourage and degrade. Lies put limits on each of us; they impede our learning and depress our soul. Lies make us feel like giving up and shame us into stagnant living. Lies eat at the meat of our life like hideous maggots. They may seem small, but they are devastating and leave behind them a trail of self-loathing carnage.

If others said unkind, mean things to us, we would avoid their association, even stop answering their calls. And yet we often allow our own minds to self-berate with cruelty and contempt. These negative thoughts are chains that render us incapable of being happy and having a positive influence on others.

The Stampede

There are times when we stand frozen in fear as we watch a herd of lies stampede through our precious lives. Lies such as:

- I couldn't bear a correction, although, if heeded, it would make me a better person.
- It is personal tragedy if someone has something that I don't have.
- The wonderful capabilities of another person somehow make less of me.
- I am not as precious as others.
- I only feel happy if I win the comparison.
- I am willing to help others, but I don't need help from them.
- I must carefully count and withhold compliments and praise.
- It would be dangerous for both of us to know how much I really love another person.
- I have no time to see through the skin of others, and I have no desire for them to see through mine.

We accept this ugly cattle-like herd of lies, and after it has trampled and destroyed, we keep it well fed. Our beasts of pride grow even stronger, but they are at our command. We can drive them back onto the range. We can then fortify our fences and close the gate.

Lean on Truth

Our youngest son, Danny, liked being cool but never wanted to be the center of attention unless it was on the basketball court. One night he went over to a friend's house to hang out with a bunch of buddies. Of course there were girls there, so he impressively sauntered into the room. Some people like to make a grand entrance, but not him. He simply wanted to be cool and casual—you know, hang back a little, maybe lean on something like a wall. Instead, he leaned against a china closet.

The top part—the hutch—was not bolted down to the bottom part. He didn't know that resting his entire handsome 6'5" frame against the hutch would begin an unstoppable disaster. He remembers seeing delicate treasures protected behind the glass doors just as he felt something give way. Then without mercy, the hutch slid and crashed onto the floor! Porcelain, window glass, crystal, and wood shattered together! There stood Mr. Cool among a heap of shards.

Thank goodness the parents of Danny's friend were there. Can you imagine trying to explain this to them? They, and everyone else, stood in a moment of silence and shock. The mother quietly left the room, saying as she walked out, "I don't even want to see anything. Just throw it away!"

The china closet had displayed antique china from Grandmother, and other precious heirlooms. Our son scrambled for pieces that matched or were large enough to glue back together. There were none. Even the wood had splintered. It was a total disaster.

Just like the hutch giving way, negative beliefs and carefully shaped lies are unstable facades that aren't bolted down. We sometimes mistakenly lean on lies of all sorts of carnal natures. They seem to be so tangible and solid, yet they slip out from beneath us.

Often we are tempted to lean on the lie that we make ourselves into someone special. Our faith in Heavenly Father and the Lord Jesus Christ fails. We shrink along with our belief in the Savior, who condescended below all, who knows firsthand about our suffering, needs, and weaknesses. Then, when in our humanness we can't perfect ourselves, we become discouraged, depressed, and angry—just as Satan wants us to be. We carelessly mock our Omnipotent Creator and Redeemer as we embrace untruths. We invite and attract personal failure.

Solid truths are always anchored. They sustain and support honest victories, and they correct misconceptions. Our Lord wants us to recognize our own true goodness. Such knowledge is a treasure that He will bestow.

In a BYU devotional, Elder David A. Bednar taught that the gift of discernment is not only to discern good or evil in others, it also helps us find and bring forth the good that may be concealed in ourselves.[1]

The eternal truth is that we are glorious and wonderful—with godly potential that exceeds our greatest dreams. We are born beautiful. We are arrayed more beautiful than the lilies of the field because we are God's daughters with the possibility of His attributes. Our empowerment comes by faith in Jesus Christ, who will lead us forward through life's tutoring course.

Another facet is cut into our diamond heart. It radiates precious love and peaceful appreciation—revealing the true identity of the real superwomen—each of us.

Notes

1. David A. Bednar, "Quick to Observe" (devotional, Brigham Young University, Provo, UT, May 10, 2005).

chapter 3

Perception Without Deception
wavy mirrors

As a child, my favorite amusement park ride was the roller coaster. Screaming and daring to throw my hands up in the air while speeding downhill in the front car was the stomach-dropping thrill of the day. That's because back in the olden days it didn't catapult me into orbital loops. It was a mild thrill. Mild was my goal.

The other rides of twirling, hammering, and shaking left me reeling with grandiose motion sickness. So I spent most of my time in the Fun House. Oh, it was a far cry from Six Flags or Disneyland, but I was delighted. I could climb up a thousand stairs, then step into a burlap bag and scream all the way down a huge slide. There were large, turning tunnels to walk through and play in. What more could such a risk-taker ask for?

One section of the Fun House had a room full of curved or wavy mirrors. Some mirrors made me look extremely tall and skinny, while others made me look short and fat. The wavy mirrors distorted my entire image. It was the best entertainment a weak-stomached child could hope for! But even as mild as it was, I loved the relief of walking out of the Fun House and into the sunlight. There I could breathe fresh air and feel sane again.

How often do we view other people through wavy mirrors? Perhaps we distort the truth in order to please our own wishes, and we refuse to see those people from a different angle or perspective.

In truth, there are times when we need an eye for the faults of others. Being a critical thinker is a vital tool. Such a thinker is neither harsh nor biased, but evaluating and considerate. As in appreciating art with its

33

texture, color, and contrast, she respectfully considers the overall tones of another person and what the value might be of a relationship. We can only accomplish this when we can mix in some logic—use our heads with our hearts. One can only think of the repercussions of dating without such open eyes, or considering a marriage proposal, accepting employment, investing money, or choosing a babysitter. Evaluations are justified and are made every day of our lives.

But, sadly, in almost every room of our lives, we find a wavy mirror. Many times the distortion is unfair and ruins our perception of the virtues of another person. We lose the ability to understand a coworker, a friend, a sibling, one of our children, or even our husband. Instead, we insist on seeing everything through our own sacred viewpoint. Instead of gripping mightily to the strong jungle vine of values and principles, we let go and reach for a little twig—a human error or frailty—that happens to catch our eye. Then we wonder why our relationships crash painfully to the ground.

The purpose of this discussion is to implore each of us to seek the beautiful and good in others—virtues that are often left undiscovered or unappreciated.

A few years ago I was sitting with my granddaughter. She was three years old and had white-blonde hair and huge brown eyes. I have no bias at all when I say she is gorgeous, smart, cute, delightful, precious, funny, darling, and perfect in every way. I looked down into her deep eyes, which magically drew every positive emotion of mine to the surface. I thought of her potential and infinite worth. I considered what she meant to me—her adoring grandma. She looked back up at me, also with consideration

As we looked into each other's eyes, she said, "Guamma?"

I replied, "Yes, darling?" I knew she was going to say something like, "You are the most wonderful guamma in the world. I love you. In fact, I wish you were my mommy! Can I stay with you forever?"

"Yes, darling, what do you want?" She could ask for anything from me, and surely it would be hers, even if it wasn't on the parent-approved list! As my sister once told me, "Grandparents and grandchildren have a common enemy—their parents."

With her tiny brows knit in seriousness came the concerned reply, "Guamma, you have boogers in your nose."

I burst out with laughter every time I remember that reality check. It reminds me that the joy of our experiences depends fully on our viewpoint.

From where are we looking? And will our viewpoint reveal delight or boogers?

Change Your Viewpoint by Changing Your Mind

The good news is that, as women, we are good about changing our minds. If you want evidence, look at the walls of my living room. Beneath a single picture are fifteen nail holes where I previously thought the picture should hang. How about your makeup bag? And think about the number of things you have in your closet that were once treasures and now take up space in the nothing-to-wear section. Every season I make a donation of clothes that my husband declares are "perfectly fine." When I call it goodwill, he gives me that knowing smile.

Changing your mind about how you look at life and what you choose to see can be the start of true joy. Changing our minds is more difficult than changing the picture on the wall or the clothes in our closets. It involves changing an attitude that we have formed through years of experiences colored by our stubborn perspective. This perspective may be a wavy mirror—never giving us a true reflection.

Is Our Autopilot Taking Us Where We Want to Go?

Our choice of attitude may come from our autopilot mechanism. Without regard or thought, we fly along on a course toward an unknown destination. It is as though we refuse to grip the wheel. We wrongly trust that our craft will at least be able to skim over the rising mountain peak looming in the distance.

Often this autopilot refuses to put down landing gear, so just below us we miss a beautiful destination. We mistakenly think our autopilot will keep us safe. After all, we have been through storms before—we have felt the injustice and unkindness of the world. We are not strangers to rejection, the pain of competition, or the loneliness of unreturned love. And so, in our automatic world, we ironically remain protected from friendship, experience, and growth.

Override the Autopilot

I could instruct myself how to feel? It was the hardest concept in the universe for me to understand! I thought it ridiculous when I was told that I chose how I felt. I thought other people made me feel certain ways. What was I supposed to do? Repeat over and over to myself, "I am happy. I am happy. I am happy"? I wanted to change how I felt, but I couldn't desert my own opinions! I wanted to hang on to them as if they were my survival.

Overriding the autopilot happens by increasing our understanding. We take control back when we decide to have an open heart and mind. We increase our ability to see an experience from a different point of view. We change our minds. We walk away from the wavy mirrors out into the sunlight. This new reference point is like an education from angels. It gives new thoughts and perceptions that enable joy when there seems to be little reason to celebrate. It helps us appreciate another person even if that person is disappointingly human.

Where once we thought we knew the truth and saw things as they really were, we now become enlightened and see beauty instead of boogers! This changes first our understanding and then our feelings about past and present experiences. Let me explain what I believe are the four prerequisites of such a personal miracle.

Prerequisite #1: Get out of where we are

Lake Powell is an enormous reservoir that fills a canyon carved by the Colorado River. It is hundreds of miles of gleaming, blue water surrounded by red rock walls of towering, magnificent strength and overwhelming beauty. It is a powerful testimony of God's creativity and love for His children. One summer, my husband and I were vacationing there on a houseboat with friends. We were basking in hundred-degree weather and wearing ourselves out from play.

Our "captain" slowly brought the houseboat to a floating stop and announced that there were ancient Indian ruins on the sheer rock to our east. We were going to climb to them, an opportunity of a lifetime! I have always been baffled by the question, "Why didn't you just stay on the boat if you were so scared?" It doesn't make any sense to me either, but I followed along, swimming to the shore. We began our ascent.

Going up was a little scary. Rocks slipped out from under my feet, but I just grabbed on to the next rock or clump of grass. Safety was only a dream to me; the mode of the moment was "Don't look back. Just keep going and you will make it."

To my credit, I did make it. The ruins were amazing—once a home to a family nestled in the hollow of rocks hundreds of feet above the ground, it had a protective view of possible enemies approaching.

It is only fair to tell you that I was actually crawling, not only because I would have bumped my head of the overhang but also because I was frightened to death! I looked over at a girlfriend of mine, who was crying. I thought perhaps she was overcome with the beauty or maybe by reverence for the past.

"Kathy?" I looked at her, wondering.

"I can't do it," she replied. "I won't be able to get out of here."

As I looked downward to the sight of a very tiny houseboat, I also became filled with terror! I contemplated the possible scenario and the ensuing headlines: Women won't budge on Lake Powell cliff. Helicopters sent to rescue.

I knew there was danger; there wasn't much to grasp in case of a slip. Slip? That would bring disaster. I also knew I had three choices: Take a step; stay there until someone knocked me unconscious and rolled me down the hill; or die on the ledge. The most excruciating step down was the first one. A heart-pounding, frightful descent continued. But somehow—well, let's say with our husbands' coaxing—we made it inch by inch!

This terrifying, trembling, and tearful experience is a thrilling memory. I wouldn't trade it for anything now.

Getting to where we are right now has been a hard, uphill climb. Our experiences haven't always been the best. We might even have some injuries—some valid reasons to stay in the ruins and pretend we are safe. We must realize that the first step out will lead us to experience thrill, awe, quiet love, and even sorrow—all better ways to respond than remaining dangerously safe.

If we want happiness and love in our lives, we must get out of the ruins. We must take the first, freaky step out onto dangerous rock and leave our fake security behind.

We are obligated to admit that we could be wrong, blinded, or just a little off. We must leave some of our opinions behind. It is the frightening step to realize that there is a different way to look at people and at life's experiences. We should risk a different viewpoint! In reality, it is wonderful to know that we have not always been right, because that also means that there is room in life for our weaknesses. We truly don't implode as we discover that we are not always right. It's just fine that no one else is always right, either. Remember, we are good at changing our minds. Isn't that comforting?

Prerequisite #2: Bridle our passions

I heard this phrase many times as I was growing up. It comes from the Book of Mormon prophet Alma, who was giving loving advice to one of his sons. Alma 38:12 reads, "And also see that ye bridle all your passions, that ye may be filled with love."

For years I thought this scripture meant only to restrain my passions, to deny myself. Now I see it differently.

I used to often jog on a dirt road along a canal. I met a woman there named Carol, who frequently rode her horse in the area. One day I asked her if she would consider giving my son his first experience on a horse. She agreed, and we planned what would be Danny's birthday present. On the morning of his birthday, I blindfolded him and drove to Carol's horse barn. When I removed the blindfold, there we stood in the barn, stalls lined on both sides and the breath of horses huffing in the cold air.

For the first time in his life, Danny was sitting on a horse! His hands clenched the saddle horn, and he pulled the reins in so tightly that the horse could only back-step. But Carol taught him to loosen up and let the horse move, and then to use the reins to guide. The entire experience took on new meaning for me: the lessons he was learning were about moving forward. We laughed while Danny's ride became fun and exciting.

To bridle our passions means to direct our passion, our focus, our emotions. We must use our bridle and reins to see the good in other people. We pull the reins of our heart in the direction of loyalty and forgiveness.

Prerequisite #3: Expect and appreciate differences.

It would be a benefit to use this advice with everyone we meet, especially in our relationships with men. I am amazed at how we women expect men to have an abundance of feminine understanding. We expect them to think like we think, to talk like we talk, to want what we want. We expect them to trade their masculine attributes for what must feel like a foreign perspective.

Many women become exhausting to their husbands. They whine and nag yet never appreciate, because they think it is his job to deliver. They cease admiring and adoring the qualities of strength that give him the ability to protect and defend. They think he is ignoring them if he doesn't listen to every detail of their day. It is as though they are looking for a girlfriend rather than a man. They have never learned or maybe have forgotten that men and women are different. We are supposed to be different. It is a blessing.

We can compare this to our political world. What is it about an ally that is so valuable? It is not that the countries are located in the same spot on earth, because the different position is an advantage. It is not that countries are common in their manufactured goods, because the difference allows beneficial trade and commerce. It isn't even that they see eye to eye on every political issue. But when allies are bound by common values, they support each other in difficult moments. Both allies not only have to tolerate and understand differences, they must also appreciate, and even adore, these differences.

One young wife told me that she had just had it with her husband's lack of romanticism. Even though he helped with their baby, went to work every day to support them, and was loyal and hardworking, he was unromantic and never complimented her! What difference could she make if she bridled her passions? What if she began to appreciate and adore what he was doing for her? And one more question: Would a million years of whining and criticism inspire him to act differently? Likely, unconditional love would be the only cure.

Shelly and Rod had been married for more than fifteen years. As husband and wife, they maintained a fair relationship, but they lacked the resonance that comes from close friendship and unity. I discussed with Shelly the importance of showing affection, concern, and love, but she held on to her resentment toward Rod. She worried about "giving in" to him, what she would lose without an argument, and the unfairness of complimenting him if he didn't compliment her. "After all," she reasoned, "I am his equal. I don't have to be his servant and answer his every desire, especially if he isn't doing his part."

Love does not keep score. It is not based on reactions but on purposeful consideration and decisive actions. I explained to Shelly that love begins in our thoughts as we consciously decide to see the good in others. We then employ the great miracle worker—kindness. It would be an enormous feat to break the score-keeping habit, but Shelly finally resolved to change.

I didn't hear from Shelly for two months. She finally called me again, this time with a different perspective. Even over the phone her excitement was obvious. "I can't believe the changes in our relationship. I feel different about him. When I began showing him more kindness, I began to feel my heart change toward him. The more kind things I thought about him, the more my feelings changed and the more my love grew.

"At first Rod didn't believe me. He seemed to doubt that I had sincere affection for him, but I just kept saying and doing sweet things. Then I started noticing my new feelings—I had actually fallen in love with him all over again! During a discussion that normally would have escalated into a fight, I could see his point of view and, surprisingly, it didn't make me angry! I learned to give him praise instead of criticism and to bite my tongue when I was tempted to change him.

"One night as we lay in bed together, I looked over at him, the soft light of the lamp on his face. I knew he was the same man I had married years ago, yet I felt different. I actually felt enlivened with that 'in-love feeling' as I leaned over to kiss him.

"Rod doesn't realize what has happened to him, but he loves it. A couple of times I have looked up to see him watching me. He smiles with tenderness that I thought had disappeared. We just feel happy together."

Shelly's thought-provoking question was, "Why did loving him become so much easier?"

Could the answer be that changing our perspective not only helps others but changes our heart and lifts our spirits? Perhaps it allows us to return to the love we once felt in the beginning. We begin to see the value in other people. They become easier to love not because they changed but because we changed. And here's the incredible bonus: Our self-love increases because we like what is happening deep in the folds of our own heart.

Women motivate men by one thing—their love. True love is not manipulating them so that we get our way. We must give love without the expecting anything in return. Thinking that we must be paid back is an assumption that not only beguiles us, but robs us of our happiness. Not all the nagging, nor even the slightest suggesting or hinting, will make a man love a woman. To the contrary, a good man is almost always a "goner" for his woman's love, acceptance, and admiration.

Prophet Joseph Smith taught, "You need not be teasing your husbands because of their deeds, but let . . . your innocence, kindness, and affection be felt . . . not war, not jangle, not contradiction, or dispute, but meekness, love, purity—these are the things that should magnify you in the eyes of all good men."[1]

One of the best assignments I have ever completed with the intent to increase my understanding and gratitude started with a list. I would practically kill myself to do a list, but instead of killing me, the actions from this list were enlivening! I received it from a wonderful professor and marriage counselor, Dr. Terry Baker, as he taught from John Gottman's book, *Why Marriages Succeed or Fail.* I like to call the list the Baker's Daily Dozen.

This powerful list created a cycle without requiring the cooperation of any other person. These actions broadened my perspective because they bridled my passions and directed my focus. This list works wonders for couples, siblings, children, friends, and coworkers. It is an all around human-loving method that helps destroy wavy mirrors.

- Copy the following list to a 3x5 card.
- Place it where you see it often.
- Memorize the list. Memorizing is extremely important because it will help you over-learn so that an idea will enter your mind when you need it.
- Consider what each direction really means—what you need to do in your daily interactions.
- Over the next week, put little marks by each item as you consciously perform that task each day.
- Continue this until these actions become your habits; then continue reading the list often to remind yourself what you need to do.

As you use this list, you will achieve change in your perspective and be blessed with a new transfusion of love and power. As others respond to your love, the magical cycle begins. You are taking part in changing the world!

Baker's Daily Dozen
1. Express fewer negatives.
2. Be less critical and cold when angry.
3. Be less defensive when listening.
4. Be an engaged listener.
5. Show interest.
6. Be affectionate.
7. Show you care.
8. Be appreciative.
9. Show your concern.
10. Be empathetic.
11. Be accepting.
12. Joke around.
13. Share your joy.

Prerequisite #4: Speak with love.

The phrase "shut up!" was never allowed in my home as a child. My sister tells a childhood story of a boy relentlessly teasing her. One day in her fierce anger, she yelled the worst thing she could think of: "Shut up!" Our family laughs about that to this day.

When in third grade, my teacher grew weary of writing my name on the board for talking. To my surprise, she walked behind me, yanked my ponytail, and yelled, "Shut up!" When I confessed to my mother, I was shocked at her response. It was the only time I know of that she went to the school to set a teacher straight, but it wasn't for pulling my hair. She boldly told that teacher never to tell me to shut up again. That's another thing our family laughs about.

Although my mother preached of the evils of saying "Shut up," there is a definite, intelligent quality of such an action, and it takes emotional maturity. To resist making a comment, to not speak the last word, to leave it be, can begin the process of understanding another's opinion and getting rid of distortion.

Sometimes withholding our own ultra-important comments will also help other people surrender their own weapons of defense. A good friend once told me, "You know, I thought if I just said it one more time, she would understand, but she didn't."

President Gordon B. Hinckley counseled,

> Criticism, faultfinding, evil speaking—these are of the spirit of our day. From many directions we are told that nowhere is there a man of integrity holding political office. Businessmen are crooks. Utilities are out to rob you. Everywhere is heard the snide remark, the sarcastic gibe, the cutting down of associates. Sadly, these are too often the essence of our conversation. In our homes, wives weep and children finally give up under the barrage of criticism leveled by husbands and fathers. Criticism is the forerunner of divorce, the cultivator of rebellion, sometimes a catalyst that leads to failure. In the Church it sows the seed of inactivity and finally apostasy.[2]

Our words can often be devastating. Once spoken, they can never be called back. They wreak havoc on understanding and friendship.

Some words have power not only to injure another person; they can also have a mesmerizing effect on ourselves. They are self-contrived lies that we embrace and then believe. They have the ability to lull us into our own emotional coma, where we excuse ourselves from self-control and the work of personal relationships.

Enjoying happiness with other people requires that instead of seeing with piercing criticism, we focus with the clarity of love. When we stop preserving our wavy, distorted pride, we experience joy. We gain the ability to accept others into our lives with gratitude and compassion.

When we give up the deception of our perception and leave condemnation behind, we gain freedom. It is the freedom of embracing, the freedom of deeply and sincerely enjoying others' worth, the freedom of expressing true love. With more ability to see others as our Savior sees them, we draw closer to Him. We walk out of dull misunderstanding into fresh air and new light. In His light, we will live with brilliant understanding and wholeness! We will live with another sparkling facet in the diamond of our heart.

Notes

1. Joseph Smith, *Teachings of the Prophet Joseph Smith*, compiled by Joseph Fielding Smith (American Fork, UT: Covenant Communications, 2002), 234.
2. Gordon B. Hinckley, "The Continuing Pursuit of Truth," *Ensign*, April 1986, 2.

chapter 4

Do What It Takes
walking the walk

When one of our sons was a daring three-year-old, he decided to ride a bike. Now what mother wants a toddler riding a bicycle? I tried to stall his experience by telling him I would help him learn in a little while. He refused to wait for help; he just wanted to ride a bike. So he would hop on his brother's old bike and pedal as best as he could. Crash after crash didn't deter his strong spirit, and before long the wobbling wheels became steady. He was riding a bike! The problem was that he just couldn't steer very well. I could barely stand to watch him zig-zag down our quiet rural street. He hit mailboxes, parked cars, and garage doors. I remember the look of panic on his face as he pedaled straight toward me—trying not to run down his own mother! We joked that he didn't know where he was going, but he sure knew where he had been.

Know Where You Want to Go

Before you begin your trek, you must know where you want to go. This is not as easy as it sounds, for numberless choices beckon, tempt, and persuade. Still, time and resources limit us, and we must make a choice. Although we are not able to do everything that appeals to us, we are able to discern what is good in a personal way that will enable us to accomplish our life's goals.

When our five children were still quite young, I decided to return to school and earn a degree in nursing. After only one semester, it was clear that my precious roles of wife and mother were being compromised by my new student role. An inner war plagued me. When I spent time on one, the other screamed in my ear, "Traitor!" Although I was never wasting time, I suffered relentless guilt. It had nothing to do with a choice between good and evil, but a choice between what was more important at that time. My nursing goal was quietly shelved.

We must be brave enough to commit ourselves to a cause. We must also be wise enough to have a cause in which our heart and mind meet together. Our walk must be of principle and commitment, with no collision of value and practice. It must be a journey of peaceful, heart-felt congruency. Our walk must be of passion combined with persistence, for without our precious emotional and physical investment, it will never be of any worth. Our walk will be that for which we are willing to cry, sigh, and die. We stake our reputation on it, and we will willingly accept the consequences.

Success in walking the walk actually lies in the doing. It is saying no at the right time so that we can say yes at the right time. When we are walking the walk, we are taking the responsibility for picking up the reins. We crack the whip high in the air, and then, with eyes wide open, we hold on for dear life.

The Powerful Heart

When we invest our heart in a goal, the stakes become high enough, increasing our willingness to do the tough stuff. It is our heart that commits us to stick to it. It is our heart that powers our dream and gives us the rhythm of our true drummer. We can use a simple acronym to remind us of vital principles for a successful walk in life:

H—Hope
E—Energy
A—Abundance of Help
R—Reward
T—Truth and Time

Hope

Hope begins with our beliefs. When we embrace a new goal, we must face our core beliefs. Imagine a war in our heart between two conflicting beliefs. In this deep and silent battle, death comes to the less trained belief. If we succumb to old ideas, they will override, and the powerful motivation of our hope will be neutralized. That is why it is important to expose the false beliefs that contradict our goals.

Hopefully, our beliefs are rooted in truth. They can be glorious and godlike. They enable progress and deepen our desire for improvement.

The way to brighten our hope is through our Savior, Jesus Christ. President Henry B. Eyring counsels,

> I was chatting with my wife at the end of a long day. Three of our children were in the room, listening. I turned and noticed that one of them was watching me—and watching my face intently. And then he asked me, softly, "Why are you unhappy?" I tried to give a reason for my furrowed brow, but I realized later that he could well have been asking this deeper question: "Can I see in you the hope for peace in this life that Jesus promised?"
>
> To turn my thoughts from what darkened my look to what would brighten it, I went to another letter from Mormon to his son. Both Mormon and Moroni were facing days of difficulty that make my challenges pale. Mormon knew his son might be overcome with gloom and foreboding, so he told him the perfect antidote. He told him that he could choose, by what he put in his mind, to become an example of hope. Here is what he wrote: "My son, be faithful in Christ; and may not the things which I have written grieve thee, to weigh thee down unto death; but may Christ lift thee up, and may his sufferings and death, and the showing his body unto our fathers, and his mercy and long-suffering, and the hope of his glory and of eternal life, rest in your mind forever" (Moroni 9:25).[1]

Acceptance and Change—The Perfect Couple. Hope is at the top of the list of attributes that will enable us to press on and accomplish goals. Alma 7:24 teaches, "And see that ye have faith, hope, and charity, and then ye will always abound in good works." Our hope hangs contingent upon the influence of the Holy Ghost, but the influence of the Holy Ghost is dependent on our ability to repent and change.

Profound doctrines of repentance are found in a passionate letter from Mormon to his son Moroni: "And the remission of sins bringeth meekness, and lowliness of heart; and because of meekness and lowliness of heart cometh the visitation of the Holy Ghost, which Comforter filleth with hope and perfect love" (Moroni 8:26).

Although repentance is part of the eighth facet, it is important to relate it to hope. When a person desires to make a change by accomplishing a goal, it is imperative to realize that the words *change* and *repentance* have great similarity and are almost synonymous. Of repentance, the Bible Dictionary states, "The Greek word of which this is the translation denotes a change of mind, i.e., a fresh view about God, about oneself, and about the world."

A fresh view of myself does not ignore what I have done. In fact, it forces me to accept the truth of my past. But it sweeps away the discouraging thought that I still need to keep doing these things! It is this fresh view that allows hope, draws me down into humility, and encourages change.

The present and the future are two opposites, but they dance beautifully together. Acceptance and change look each other in the eye. Acceptance leads out with a starting point and a desire to be better; change follows. This couple is meant to be together. They speak eternal truths back and forth, dancing to eternal choreography and pace. The wonderful part is that this isn't a fairy tale. The clock never strikes midnight. We are never doomed. As long as we stay in the dance, it is never over, because the dance goes on.

Making Our Own Misery or Music—"For as he thinketh in his heart, so is he" (Proverbs 23:7). Within themselves, people often repeat remarks of unkindness and merciless judgments. Their self-sabotage includes suicidal stabbings of self-respect, the robbing and plundering of fresh hope, and the suffocation of change.

It is possible to change our feelings of low esteem—by changing our thoughts. I continue to be astounded by the effect of what we say to ourselves. Honesty compels its examination in every facet of our lives.

Dr. Dean W. Belnap, a fellow of the American Psychiatric Association, a member of the clinical faculty at the University of Utah Medical School, and in the private practice of child neuropsychiatry stated,

> Whatever thoughts or behaviors you have imprinted yourself, or have allowed others to imprint on your brain, are affecting, directing or controlling everything about you. . . .
>
> Inner speech is a remarkable level of brain functioning found only in the human mind. . . .
>
> With inner speech we give new direction to our minds by talking to ourselves in a different way. We can consciously re-program our prefrontal cortex with words and statements that are more effective and help with improving ourselves and creating new imprints. Inner conversation can paint a new internal picture of us: What we would like to be, we can be. . . .
>
> The concept of positive thinking is a good start. Unfortunately, such help is temporary unless we have programmed our minds to go beyond

just condemning the negative. Making a decision to never again think negatively, and for the rest of our lives think positively, while it may work for a time, cannot last. Why? Because the mental imprints still sit deep in our minds. They have to be replaced [b]y new imprints, new ways of seeing and saying things. If we tell ourselves that from today onward we will never again think negatively, without at the same time giving ourselves a specific new word vocabulary of the positive things to say to ourselves, we will soon slip back to the old habit of thinking negatively.[2]

Dr. Belnap explains that we must identify our inner speech by writing down the negative experiences, moods, situations, and labels we use to stereotype and depress ourselves. In their place, substitute written hopeful statements and avoid dwelling on past and forgiven problems.

> You may have to command yourself to stop! . . . . Add images to your mind that are positive for ideas or memory. . . .
>
> Wanting to be a positive thinker is not enough. Making the decision to have a positive attitude is not enough. Our mind says: "Give me more, give me the words, give me the directions, the commands, the picture, the schedule, and the results you want." . . . "Feast upon the words of Christ" and He will give you the "words." Educate and program your mind by searching the scriptures. . . . No one else has that right.[3]

We enliven our hope by refusing to repeat the degrading notions and phrases we may be accustomed to hearing from ourselves. We replace them with well-thought-out expressions from the word of God. These directives write a new tune in our souls, then motivate us with the truth of who we are meant to be. We memorize a new song and dance.

I have heard arguments such as, "That is so 'not me' to say such positive, good things to myself," "I think it's embarrassing!" and "You've got to be joking!" But experience teaches me this is true.

※

I had the shakes. It was my first math class in twenty-five years. I had to force myself to open the classroom door. How lucky—no one else had arrived! I guess young students don't show up twenty minutes early for class like a forty-six-year-old granny. I didn't sit in the front row. Give me a break! I know that is so nerdy. I sat in the second row.

When the professor walked into the classroom, it reminded me of meeting my doctor. Much too young to be so smart. She looked me in the eye and tweaked out a half smile. I was probably the only one in the class who had already purchased the text. Talk about prepared! I brought cute mechanical pencils (seven of them, actually), notebooks, bifocal reading glasses, gum to help me stay awake, and even a backpack. I had never owned a backpack until my husband took me school shopping the way we used to take our kids.

I glanced around the room. The other students were about as old as my babies, and I was in their math class! In the same moment I wanted to vomit, scream, and run. Lies about my ability started creeping into my mind—my incompetence, my ridiculous goal of being a college graduate, and my old middle age. Still, a slim light of hope edged through the closing door, and I told myself that these children had nothing over on me in the brain department. After all, I had raised five children—somewhat like them—and I had outsmarted each of those five many times over the years! Of course I still had the professor to convince.

I hoped that I could get an A out of the class. I realized there are three great advantages to being an old, married lady returning to college: I didn't have to be cool, I didn't have to get a date, and I might get six hours of sleep each night.

I talked to myself the entire semester about my new math ability, my dedication to study, and my growing understanding. I read in the scriptures that the Holy Ghost could bear the truth of all things. I prayed for an open mind that would actually shut in time to retain facts. Making an action plan, I asked more questions than anyone else and did more than twice the homework. The semester ended and my belief survived—I earned my A.

I didn't simply make naive, positive comments to myself. I actually made a plan, gave myself directions, and then followed a homework schedule. I knew the Holy Ghost would help me achieve my utmost potential. It wasn't self-talk that did the actual work, but it was self-encouragement that bolstered my motivation.

Hope is state-of-the-art being! It is accepting the fact that there are wonderful possibilities. Hope includes our discontent and is born of a desire to change. It is the essence of nudging life forward. Hope is often uncomfortable because it requires teetering on the unknown. It is not merely wishing, because it requires care and attention. It shoulders us with the responsibility of decision. It offers us a mountain to climb. It tells us that along with our mortal birth came the birth of opportunity and agency.

Hope embraces the universal truth that change is eminent and we are empowered to effect the change—to influence and even direct its course. Hopefulness is not a blind journey of disrespect for adversity, but the embrace of difficult times along with the less challenging. It begins at this moment!

Energy

We have all been invigorated when we have been able to put our heart into something. Imagine that the power created in your heart—the turbine of your soul—is surging round and round. Sadly, this energy can be misdirected or even diffused. It can seep out into the universe, never bringing joy or strength. At the same time, you can direct this power to truly create possibilities and sustain quality in your life.

Have you ever visited a hydroelectric dam? There are channels through which the water can push and turn the turbine. This produces enough power to light cities! If you look on the back side of the dam, you see the possibility of power, a large body of water pressing against the barriers, searching for direction.

Consider life and ambition without man-made dams. My family lived in Idaho Falls at the time the Teton Dam broke. A wall of 80 billion gallons of water went crashing through cities, submerging the steeple of a church, engulfing and pushing buildings and homes as though they were children's toys. It tore out trees and washed away tons of fertile top soil. The houses that were recovered didn't resemble what the owners had known. In place of beloved treasures and furniture were knee-deep layers of mud and sludge. For more than fifty miles, the effects of undirected energy wrought havoc and devastation.

Needless suffering can occur in our lives if we don't reserve and channel our energy. We will be left uprooted, shoveling our own deposits of mud and sludge. Just as devastating is the little trickle, wandering in a path of least resistance. We tolerate it, but it can never give us much power.

Each of us has set a worthy goal and then fallen short. How do we erect a dam to keep our energy flowing? The answer is, with focused determination! This sort of commitment may bring you the reputation of a fanatic, but that's exactly what you need to be if you want to reach a difficult goal! Casual consideration will only get you a useless trickle.

Focused determination plugs leaks that can otherwise drain our energy. At the beginning of a new day, we can start with a focus on our goal and then ask, "What's going to turn my turbine today?" Other questions might be, "How can I make restitution today?" and "What can I do that will restore my emptiness, quench my longing, and bring me closer to my goal?"

The answers to these questions can be very revealing! It's not our goal that keeps us focused; every day we must generate control over our goal! We envision success and how it will feel. We think of the misery we will feel if we don't stick to it. We realize that what we may have called "no big deal" really does matter. We resolve to answer the questions with plans and actions.

There may be weak spots—places in our dam that could give way or burst. Accomplishment requires investigation, repair, and fortification. These are parts of our daily plan that may include something as simple as removing obstacles or temptation. Or it could involve changing a circumstance or ritual, or receiving encouragement from a mentor. Just keep going. Get up every morning and do it again. If you quit, you shut the gate of opportunity; the light dims, then flickers, and finally blacks out. On the other hand, if you perform daily tasks and work toward your dream, energy flows through you. Momentum is on your side.

Abundance of Help

The moment we begin to change is the moment we have to admit that there really are monsters under the bed. It is the moment when we startle the universe of opposition. It is as though sleeping beasts awaken and sniff us out. They attempt to frighten us back into the caves of our pasts, places where we felt protected but were dying from a lack of light. These beasts are magnificently groomed but are powerless when we arise and take command. It may seem impossible, but from somewhere deep inside is revealed the ability to be more than the beast. We have the power to step into the unknown darkness to find a place where a saving light begins to shine.

We often experience our greatest joy after passing through our deepest sorrow. Adopting the prideful attitude that we need no help along the way is a grave mistake. Accounts in the Book of Mormon warn of this danger: "Now, the Lamanites knew nothing concerning the Lord, nor the strength of the Lord, therefore they depended upon their own strength" (Mosiah 10:11). This attitude led to destruction.

As we know, profound is the life of a person who accepts the Atonement of Jesus Christ. I was once instructed that everything we ask for is essentially asking for relief from the fall of our first parents. Our weaknesses, both great and small, are a sure part of our mortal existence. It is the natural man whose veins flow with impurity, whose desires are carnal, who "underst[ands] not the dealings of the Lord" (Mosiah 10:14), and who must rely on the grace of our Redeemer.

Only Christ can make up for our insufficiencies. It is He alone who strengthens and nurtures. Elder Jeffrey Holland taught in the April 2006 General Conference that we should make whatever changes we can. "Whatever you may need," he counseled, ". . . come first to the gospel of Jesus Christ."[4]

The Lord's promises are clear and sure: "But they that wait upon the Lord shall renew their strength; they shall mount up with wings as eagles; they shall run, and not be weary; and they shall walk, and not faint" (Isaiah 40:31). And "Fear thou not; for I am with thee: be not dismayed; for I am thy God: I will strengthen thee; yea, I will help thee; yea, I will uphold thee with the right hand of my righteousness" (Isaiah 41:10). Aren't these amazing promises as we work toward our goals?

Leaning on the Lord will also lead us to those who are willing to give us exactly what we need. Our prayers for help are often answered by our fellow men. If we have never found such abundance, it is only because we are refusing to see it.

David Whyte writes about experiencing this shift in paradigm in one of his experiences in the Himalayas. He had decided to follow a different route than his climbing buddies' and then meet up with them at a rendezvous point. He had been immersed in beauty and solitude when he came to an immense black gorge. Standing on a grassy shelf, he gazed across the chasm. To his utter dismay, the bridge across the chasm was broken. He writes,

> The taut metal cables on one side of the narrow footbridge had snapped and the old rotted planks that made up its floor had concertined into a crazy jumble in the middle. Looking down through the gaps, I could see the dizzying three-or-four hundred-foot drop into the dark lichened gorge below.
>
> I stopped right by the very entrance step to the bridge, calculated the movements I would have to make—a kind of entangled tightrope walk at full stretch between the two remaining cables on the left-hand side of the bridge—

David started as if to cross, then retreated to a safe rock. He continues,

> After the hour had passed I had finally faced up to defeat, made an attempt to swallow my pride, and determined that there was nothing for

it but to shoulder my pack and start back down the path. As I reached for my pack, I noticed the silhouette of a small but strangely shaped figure shuffling into view along the same cliff path that had brought me to the bridge. I saw her but she did not see me. An old bent woman, carrying an enormously wide-mouthed dung basket on her back, she saw nothing but the ground she was so intent on searching. In these bare high places, denuded of trees and fuel, yak dung dries quickly in the parched air and is harvested as a valuable fuel.

She shuffled, head bent, toward me, and seeing at last the two immense booted feet of westerner, looked up in surprise. Her face wrinkled with humor as she registered her surprise, and in the greeting customary throughout Nepal, she bowed her head toward me with raised hands, saying, "Namaste." The last syllable held like a song. "I greet the God in you."

I inclined my head and clasped my hands to reply, but before I could look up, she went straight across that shivering chaos of wood and broken steel in one movement. I saw her turn for a moment, smile almost mischievously, and then to my astonishment, she disappeared from the sunlight into the dripping darkness of the opposing cliff.

Incredulous, but without for one moment letting myself stop to think, I picked up my pack and went straight after her, crossing the broken bridge in seven or eight quick but frightening strides.[5]

You may find yourself frozen at the edge of a cliff, wondering what your next step should be. If you will be patient, help will come. It may not be what you were hoping for or expecting, but it will assuredly result in what you need. You can take the step until you successfully navigate the chasm.

Reward

We deserve to celebrate every day of our lives! When do we know we have succeeded? Is it when we are perfect? Will there be an epitaph engraved on our headstone proclaiming, "Almost happy"? We must break the pattern of focusing on what we consider to be our failures!

Often we are incapable of discerning between success and failure. Many times we deceive ourselves by deeming our efforts unsuccessful. Although many experiences don't turn out the way we wish, they hold great value on our learning curve. True success requires multiple attempts and corrections, even adjustments of a goal.

If all we feel along the way to our goal is misery and longing for the end, how long will we want to stick to our path? The fun is not simply reaching the end of the journey; it's also in reaching the mile markers along the way.

✳

One spring my husband and I went to visit our grandchildren in Washington. In anticipation of our time together, my six-year-old granddaughter asked me if I would participate in a fun-run sponsored by the city. I was delighted.

She proudly confided in me, "Well, Grandma, you know we will win. If we run together we can beat everyone!"

The pressure was on and the race began. We had not even gone a block when little Madeline started whining about how difficult it was—how thirsty she was, how her legs hurt!

I said, "Maddie, should we just stop now? If we do, it's all right with me."

"No, Grandma! We can't stop."

We continued running. Maddie never let go of my hand. But her whining turned into full-blown crying out loud! Several times I said, "Maddie, should we stop?"

She would answer, "Oh, Grandma! I really hate this, but let's keep going."

Other runners would pass us and look at me as if I were a child abuser. One woman ran up to me and said, "You know, winning this race doesn't mean that much to me. You can go ahead, and I will stay back with the little girl."

I practically shriveled with embarrassment that someone thought I was dragging this crying six-year-old with me trying to win. I replied to the lady, "Well, I'm really not forcing her to do this. I don't care about winning. She wants to keep running!"

The woman was still attentive to Maddie's complaints and crying. She looked at Maddie's sweaty little head and then at me with condemning disbelief. I knew what we must look like, so I couldn't blame her.

At one point in the race we had finally made it up quite a long, difficult hill. It was a hard run—especially when holding hands with a six-year-old. When we reached the summit, I stopped and dropped Maddie's hand. I put my hands on her shoulders and turned her little body around to see the distance we had come.

"Look where we have been and, darling, look where we are!"

We had come so far and made so many twists that our starting point wasn't visible. But we could see the magnificent hill we had just conquered.

Maddie looked for a moment, and then that little tear-stained, sweaty face actually celebrated. She laughed out loud. I took a cup of water from the aid station and poured it over our heads. Maddie had her second wind, and we finished the race.

Later that day, we went to the awards ceremony at the pavilion at the park. I had no idea who had won the race in Maddie's age group, but she completely expected a first-place ribbon. To my amazement her name was called over the loud speaker as the first-place runner in her age bracket!

I was thrilled for Maddie's success in her own personal marathon! We all screamed and cheered as she proudly ran up to accept her prize. Moments later, while we were fussing over her—kissing, hugging, and taking pictures—I heard my name called over the loud speaker. There must not have been any other grandmas in the race, because I won first place in my age bracket! I wanted to shoot myself rather than go up to the pavilion and accept a prize, but Maddie was likewise thrilled and proud of me.

As I hurried to the front to get my ribbon, I came face to face with the unsympathetic woman who had no conception of what had happened. All I could do was smile as she shook her head and gave me a look like, "Some people."

Today I have a picture on my refrigerator of Maddie and me with our first-place ribbons. Allow me to tell you what really remains in Maddie's heart. Several months later, I traveled again to visit her family. All eight of us were having a bonding moment, riding in the minivan, when Maddie exclaimed, "Grandma, there's our hill!"

From my back-seat position between car seats, I looked out at our sacred summit—special only to those who knew.

Maddie's medal had long since found its way to the bottom of her toy box. Still, the memory of appreciating the journey—that moment of our greatest joy—remained in her heart. It underscored the importance of stopping to realize where we have been and celebrating each segment of our lifelong journey. Rewards can be quite simple, yet such celebrating makes our minor victories fun and allows us to proclaim our gratitude for precious, everyday life.

Truth and Time

When we use truth as a foundation for our goals, we are protected and guided by our Heavenly Father. He knows and loves us best. Helaman reminded us, "And now, my sons, remember, remember, that it is upon the rock of our Redeemer, who is Christ, the Son of God, that ye must build your foundation; that when the devil shall send forth his mighty winds, yea, his shafts in the whirlwind, yea, when all his hail and his mighty storm shall beat upon you, it shall have no power over you to drag you down to the gulf of misery and endless wo, because of the rock upon which ye are built, which is a sure foundation, a foundation whereon if men build they cannot fall" (Helaman 5:12).

We have the privilege of praying for help from the Author of Truth, and if we have real intent, He will send it. His cause will become our cause.

Having real intent is more than having a desire for help; it is our intention to be obedient. I am positive that I have missed out on many answers to my prayers because of my lack of intent to obey whatever answer the Lord provided. Sometimes I have simply kept praying, trying to get the answer I desired.

After our diligent obedience and our commitment to obey further promptings, we will receive divine inspiration. Our Heavenly Father wants us to win our battles of change. He wants us to become more like His son, to have Christ's image in our countenance.

Our willing heart can express the desire to walk the walk of truth—to accept God's will for our life. But to know the truth and to want additional truth are two different things. When goodness and virtue are our intentions, when deep within we want what He wants, we are happy, peace-filled, and strengthened.

If we envy falsehood but want to change, He can help us. But we can't simply remain idle. We must begin our walk as though we already had a committed heart. With each mile comes a witness of the truth of what we are doing, and we receive nourishment for the next mile. This is the process of nourishing a testimony.

We don't begin finished. We don't even make it midway finished. But the first few steps—hard and difficult as they might be—create the momentum for the next milepost. Certainly, times of testing will ask us to lead out in uncertainty. Choosing what we believe to be true and then walking in that direction helps us know if we made the right choice. If it is wrong, hypocrisy will stir our hearts and we will be given the opportunity to turn around. Our decision to do so validates the risk.

Walking our walk requires that we be true to promises—that we take our covenants seriously. Our ability to do this is magnified by our love for those who are deeply important to us. We prove with every partial mile that we can be trusted, especially when things get difficult. We trudge through lashing storms because we have the vision of integrity, self-respect, and love. Although the journey may be treacherous, we are protected by heaven's promises and powers.

Change is not found at the drive-up window. We can't step up to the counter and order life "our way" and then expect everything to be freshly grilled in time to get to our next appointment. We can't have a quality life without putting in the quantity of time.

In our slowing down, we have a chance to notice what we are becoming. That is a remarkable experience! Slowing down allows us to appreciate the simple blessings that mean everything to us. We are trained to cope with deadlines, dates, and appointments. They may be necessary, but they can have an unfair influence on how we feel about ourselves. We are prone to get in fast forward mode, and sometimes we miss the entire conversation of life.

Time will allow us to serve others with our newfound talents—even while we are still engraining them in our hearts. This service will embed our change even deeper. It will allow us to retain our more perfected state—the remission of our sins. In the scriptures we read, "And now, for the sake of these things which I have spoken unto you—that is, for the sake of retaining a remission of your sins from day to day, that ye may walk guiltless before God—I would that ye should impart of your substance to the poor, every man according to that which he hath, such as feeding the hungry, clothing the naked, visiting the sick and administering to their relief, both spiritually and temporally, according to their wants" (Mosiah 4:26).

The world is starving for our examples and service. If we take time to live, love, and give, we can enjoy the miraculous blessings of the Atonement.

At the moment of decision, we are required to walk a different walk. A portion within us begs to shrink. It seeks comfort and a compliance with our surroundings. It leans to making peace with predictable traditions and futures. The other portion seeks for a better way, one that challenges us with curiosity and hope.

Our greatest problem is that we don't rely on the Atonement of Jesus

Christ to effect change. As Elder Jeffrey Holland testified in his conference address in April 2006, "He [Christ] knows the way out and He knows the way up. He knows it because He has walked it."[6] Others may inspire us to improve and to magnify our talents, but only through the Atonement can we experience permanent changes.

Change is not a showy parade of our accomplishments. It is a walk, with real intent, that leads us to a sacred summit. A time will surely come when we will pause and look back. With surprise, we will realize that with divine help we have fought a good fight, finished our course, and kept the faith (2 Timothy 4:7). From the splendor of another facet, we will never be the same again.

Notes

1. Henry B. Eyring, *To Draw Closer to God* (Salt Lake City: Deseret Book, 2004), 132–33.
2. Dean W. Belnap, "A Brain Gone Wrong: The Essence of Agency," *Meridian*, October 2007, http://www.meridianmagazine.com/ideas/050322brain5.html.
3. Ibid
4. Jeffrey R. Holland, "Broken Things to Mend," *Ensign*, May 2006, 69.
5. David Whyte, *The Heart Aroused* (New York: Doubleday, 1994), 47–51.
6. Holland, "Broken Things to Mend," in Conference Report, Apr. 2006.

chapter 5

Remember Who You Are
your tie to divinity

*R*emember who you are!" Mother always stood at the door and gave me that memorable good-bye. It meant several things, depending on my age at the time:

- Don't call anyone a bad name.
- Be quiet when your teacher is talking.
- It's okay to be different—you should be different.
- Do your own work.
- You're beautiful without all that makeup.
- I love you.
- Homecoming queen isn't everything.
- Heavenly Father loves you.
- You have better things to do.
- You are important.
- Say your prayers, just like you've been taught.
- See, you did live through childbirth.
- Just love the people around you.

Quite an impressive list, incomplete as it is. Remembering who we are means honoring our potential by having a clear understanding of our origin. We can talk all day about our DNA, and we can discover, appreciate, or lament traits that have been passed to us from past generations. We respond to the influence of our communities, which gives us an understanding of our identity.

Who we are is also influenced by things that began in another sphere before our birth—a world we don't remember. Perhaps you have felt a longing, but have not understood what for. Elder Neal A. Maxwell expressed his understanding of this feeling: "May each of us, brothers and sisters, navigate that straight and narrow way, landing our immortal souls 'at the right hand of God in the kingdom of heaven' (Helaman 3:30). Only then, when we are really home, will our mortal homesickness disappear—our highest human yearnings for what could be are but muffled memories of what once was—and will again be—for we have indeed 'wandered from a more exalted sphere' (Hymns, no. 138.)"[1]

Though the curtain is drawn across our memory, we are not left without assurance. Through the Holy Ghost, all things can be brought to our remembrance (John 14:26)—including the fact that we are children of God. We can count on our Heavenly Father for strength, emotional rescue, and unqualified love.

Call to Him

The tropical breeze whispered across the water as we listened to the waves beat against the shore. The smell of sand, sea, and island flowers magically soothed every nerve.

Hoping this was not a dream, I opened my eyes. Sure enough, I was looking out across the beautiful Pacific. We lay on the white sands of Breneke—a long, narrow, cove-like beach surrounded by ominous black lava rock. Animated white spray exploded over the lava as the ocean pounded with unrelenting, powerful force. I smiled gratefully as I watched my husband, Al, stretch out on his mat and then relax as his normal cares dissolved into the humid air.

For the first time in our lives we had walked the seashore together. The overwhelming vastness of the great ocean gave me a sense of being part of a larger universe. From somewhere far away we might appear as tiny, insignificant dots. A little whisper deep within my soul told me that somehow I was important. I was warmed to my core—not only by the sun's penetrating rays but with newfound gratitude that Al and I could be insignificant and slightly important together.

I belonged to someone I loved, and he loved me. As I saw it, we were a perfect couple living a perfect day. Our love was a gift from God.

We had traveled to Kauai with four other couples and had just begun our ten-day dream vacation. The waves at Breneke were perfect for our small-time surfing. We would paddle out on boogie boards, wait for just the right wave, and ride in until we beached on our stomachs. We played like children, with no constraint of time, laughing and screaming and doing the same wonderful thing over and over again.

One thing I am not is a swimmer. But with the help of the buoyant water and my boogie board, I felt brave . . . at least a little brave. Besides, with our friends, everything was fun and thrilling. I didn't know how quickly thrill could change to terror, but I was about to discover the deceit of ocean water and remember, once again, my insignificance.

During our swim, we were all in a row, trying to catch a wave and race to shore. I was on the end. Next to me was our friend Kim, a husky football player–type man, then Al and the rest of our group. I was only a few feet from Kim when Al called for me to swim closer to the group. I smiled at his concern, which was justified since he was privy to my incompetent water skills. But I just waved and with a little laugh said, "Hon, I'm just right here. I'm fine."

"Mary, get over here!" Al called. "Closer!"

I began to paddle toward my husband. At least I tried to move toward him.

"Mary! Now! Get over here now!"

Exasperated by my feeble attempt to swim to them, Kim assured Al, "Hey, I'm right here. I'll help her."

By now, even though I had been paddling hard, I was several more yards away from the group. At that moment I saw a huge wave rolling toward me. Crash!

I tumbled in the water, gripping the rope of the boogie board as though it were my only lifeline. I came up choking in time to see another wave about to break.

My rule about not putting my head under water had definitely been broken! I was amazed at the depth of the water, how long I stayed under, and how hard I fought to get back to the surface. When I did, I saw Kim. He comforted me with a laugh and shouted, "Can you believe this?" Another wave hit us and we were both driven down into the depths, never touching the ocean floor.

I knew I was in trouble when Kim wasn't smiling. He was yelling chopped up phrases between the breaking waves.

I had two things going for me: a boogie board and my physical condition as a runner. I kept thinking, *If I can just hold on to this board, then I can hold on to my life.* The waves hit faster, but after being thrown and smashed into the water, we came up, grabbed a breath, then exerted every ounce of energy in an effort to swim toward safety. Caught in the undertow, we were unable to move more than a couple of feet.

In the turbulence of the ocean, I lost the boogie board. Kim was still trying to get over to me. By now we were within fifty yards of being dashed to pieces on the lava rock. He yelled, "Swim away from the rocks!"

Swim? I was *trying* to swim! My shoulders ached, and my throat and eyes burned. My legs couldn't muster another kick. A desperate desire for survival came over me as I thought about my children and husband—our unfinished moments. It was not about what I had done, but what I had not done. I knew that if it were left to my own strength, my unprepared life would be over.

I then found myself praying.

As a child, I had been taught of a God of miracles, a God of love. I had been raised by a mother who read me scriptures and, even against my wishes, required me to read them aloud to her. I had been taught to pray with intent, and I knew a personal God—not some vague presence in the heavens, but a Heavenly Father who knew my name. I hoped he would answer my prayer.

"Oh, Heavenly Father, I just need a little rest. Then I can hang on. Just a little rest."

In the next instant I was surrounded by a miracle. There was no wave rolling toward me. In the ocean deep, my feet touched a floor of sand! I actually stood still and every muscle spoke gratitude. I filled my lungs with air instead of water!

Seeing Kim a few yards away, I screamed, "Kim! Over here! I can touch!"

Kim was able to reach me to share his board, but then it was over. The next wave hit. Even so, I had rested, felt strengthened, and was miraculously sustained until help came.

My hopes took a giant leap when I saw Al running and jumping on the lava—waving. He pointed to our rescuers—scrawny, native teenage boys, equipped with fins and boogie boards velcroed to their wrists. Like a sick whale, I was towed to shore. My life was spared by a miracle—a direct answer to my prayer. I would always know that I called upon my Heavenly Father and He knew my needs and came to my rescue.

Many times in life we need saving. We are tossed and pounded by problems, trauma, or sorrowful loneliness. Sometimes from the gully of failure where we lay bleeding from a nasty fall, we question our worth, our influence, and our small and sorry impact. Relief comes as we remember who we are—children of an all-knowing and all-loving God—and we call to Him. Through our reliance and willingness, the answer to our prayer will be one of our miracles—our testimony.

Calling to Heavenly Father requires as little as a simple desire to believe He is there (see Alma 32:27). As a tiny seed of faith is nourished, it has the potential to grow and develop into a testimony that enriches and empowers, "springing up in you unto everlasting life" (Alma 33:23). A testimony is more than a nice thing to have; it is the power to be happy.

Elder Richard G. Scott proclaims, "A strong testimony is the unshakable foundation of a secure, meaningful life where peace, confidence, happiness and love can flourish. . . . A strong testimony is the sustaining power of a successful life. It is centered in an understanding of the divine attributes of God our Father, Jesus Christ and the Holy Ghost. It is secured by a willing reliance upon Them."[2]

***

During a few years of our married life, Al served as the bishop of a single's ward. How we loved those "kids" as they became part of our lives. We not only shared solemn and important experiences but also had great fun together. I was asked to speak in their Relief Society. My assigned topic? How to be happy.

I wrestled with this topic. To think I could actually tell someone how to be happy seemed ridiculous. I told one of my good friends about my struggle. I said, "I don't know why I am so happy. It's just inside me."

She replied to me with quick candor, "You're so happy because you're so dumb! You never have a clue if someone is upset with you. You have no idea if someone doesn't like you. In fact, you don't even know when you've offended someone!"

We laughed together, and I thought I knew what she meant.

I have enjoyed happiness all of my life, but it has never come from worldly possessions. Contemplation offers me the following explanation for my happiness.

Like times before, I headed across the driveway. The warm sun infused the unsettled dust as it flirted with the gravel. Vigilant to the sandburs, my bare feet carefully picked a path to my father's shop. I stopped abruptly at the tall wooden door surrounded by the dark, rough cinder blocks. There, in a little weed patch, was a glorious surprise of miniature purple daisies. I gleefully gathered them up. I dusted their grainy roots and held them up for inspection. Their tiny, sunny heads and green lacy leaves fit perfectly in my small, tanned fist.

Taking hold of the hot, metal doorknob, I huffed in determination to open it. This time, with one hand wrapped around my treasure, I was unable to move the heavy door. From inside, the knob turned and the door swung open, revealing the most handsome man in the world! There he stood, looking at least double 6'2" frame—majestic, as if he were king of the universe! A strand of his dark, wavy hair hung down across an indent from a welding hood that circled his head. He smiled and with a deep, short chuckle, held out his arms.

I fell—no, I was pulled—into the man's warm, greasy coveralls. With a tender heart completely wide open, I felt an ocean of love splash over me. It then receded, leaving me with a perfect memory. After his hug, I drew in a breath that filled my nostrils with welding smoke and motor fumes.

I held the flowers out to him, like an offering, a token, a promise. He held out his hand to receive. His hands. Every cut and crease was puttied and smoothed with black grease. With movie-star charisma, he took the daisies and carefully put them in a can. Then, with great drama, he placed it carefully on display among the clanging heaps of tools, hardware, and machinery.

During dinner I heard my father's lively, opinionated political discussions and insights into the gospel. At night I rode his bouncing knee, listened to his humorous songs, and shared his bowl of ice cream.

That summer, as God continued with His plan—which I was ironically promised would someday bring great joy—my father started to die. One day Mama called me. "Mary, Daddy wants to see you. Take this plate of chocolate cake and feed it to him."

The door of Father's bedroom was opened for me and there lay my king of the universe, finally bedridden. His quilt flowed across him like a blanket of snow up to his armpits, and he was propped on pillows to greet me.

Sitting down on the side of his bed, I fed him bites and giggled when the frosting got on his cheek or crumbs spilled down his neck. As I left his side, he said again what he had said a million times: "I love you, Mary."

I left the room in childish innocence, thinking that I would hear his voice a million more times.

Not many days later, I was sent to the front yard to watch for an ambulance. I looked down the street. Fearless. Ignorant. Anxious. Anticipating. Then flashing red lights came screaming over the hill. Too young to be witnesses of such tragedy, my three-year-old brother and I were ushered across the street to stay with a neighbor. Several hours later, we stood at the street again, this time to cross back into a completely different life. It was a life without a father who provided for his family, a life without a knee to bounce on, a life without funny songs or a shared bowl of ice cream.

When I walked into the house, all I could see were men's back pockets and ladies' big bottoms. Were there no faces anywhere? I couldn't even find Mama. I called out loud, "Did Daddy die?" The doctor, a family friend, picked me up. He held me in his arms and as carefully as possible wounded my heart with the finalities of what had been my security and love.

I didn't want to cry; I wanted to beg God—whoever He was. I wanted to call for help. I wanted to talk to someone really smart. In childlike grief, I watched the only tears I was ever to cry for Daddy in my entire childhood. They came quietly, one drop at a time, onto my soft, small arm.

I bid my father a strange good-bye at the funeral home. Mama took my hand in her own and placed it on Daddy's forehead. With control and fervor, she said, "He is cold because he is not in there. But don't you worry, he has gone to live with Jesus, and we will be with him someday."

When sympathetic friends arrived, I matter-of-factly escorted their daughter to my father's casket as if to teach a science lesson. There I saw his grease-stained hands unnaturally positioned across his chest, and I defied association between that corpse and my father. With stoic resolution, I testified to my friend, "Don't worry. My daddy really isn't in there. He has gone to live with Jesus, and I will be with him someday."

The Holy Ghost bore witness to me, a little, insignificant six-year-old, that what my mother told me was absolute truth. From then on, I owned the precious luxury of a testimony of the plan of salvation. Indeed, I was a child of God. My conviction of the truth of life after death and of an involved, passionate Heavenly Father was strengthening. This spiritual connection gave me dignity instead of despair. It sustained me through the difficult years and my desperate longing for a father.

Happiness was not shelved for better times. Mother was gifted with the talent to make every day worth living. Because of the immeasurable blessings of the gospel, my future was secure. As Alma promised, my burdens were indeed made light (see Alma 33:23).

＊

If I could again speak to the single's ward about how to be happy, I would know what to say because I have recognized the source: your testimony, which will sustain you when a job is harder than you ever dreamed it would be or when your heartbreak feels so deep that you can't imagine healing. Your testimony is your tie to Divinity. It empowers you to stay committed to your family. It gives you the relief of forgiving others and allows you to climb out of deep holes. It will give you power to live your dream. Without a testimony, you cannot reach your true potential.

A Divine Heritage

We are Heavenly Father's literal spirit children. Speak the words out loud: "Heavenly Father." These words imply something different from the holy name God. We say "Heavenly Father" as a child—no matter our age—a child asking for direction, for help, and for the ability to feel love. Think of how we pray. We call out, "Heavenly Father," with reverence, worship, and faith. With the words "Heavenly Father," we declare our inheritance and hope of a glorious future.

Grace, my four-year-old granddaughter, bowed her head to pray. She began, "Heavenly Father . . ."

She suddenly stopped, looked upward, and yelled, "Helloooo! Are you there?"

Oh yes, Grace, He is there!

That we have a literal relationship with our Maker is more than simply saying so. It is a truth not only handed down through the ages but revealed by modern prophets to the entire world.

In "The Family: A Proclamation to the World," we are taught, "All human beings—male and female—are created in the image of God. Each is a beloved spirit son or daughter of heavenly parents, and, as such, each has a divine nature and destiny. . . . In the premortal realm, spirit sons and daughters knew and worshiped God as their Eternal Father and accepted His plan by which His children could obtain a physical body and gain earthly experience to progress toward perfection and ultimately realize his or her divine destiny as an heir of eternal life."[3]

This revelation fills my soul with gratitude! It removes all the guesswork and all my wondering about personal worth. It instills purpose and a desire to endure all things because I am heir to an unfathomable fortune.

Trust in Eternity

For some, this is too good to be true. On the one hand, we have the hope from these words that we are beloved children of a Heavenly Father and Mother, and we have a divine destiny! This hope may bring us only to the verge of what we know will be such extensive, penetrating joy that our longing and searching is finally able to rest. Even so, we dare not let go of the finite and the tangible.

Perhaps pride ruins our faith. We feel awkward or too childish. We might be feeling, "God may be there, but His love has always seemed to be a few inches out of reach. Look at my history. It is proof that I have done it myself. He has not saved me from misery or pain."

Maybe we stop short because we don't feel able to embrace something so perfect for ourselves. It may not even be disbelief, but rather we just won't do the work.

Many of us use the excuse that we will not believe in a God who allows suffering or the torturous injustices of our world. I do not pretend to understand the suffering of the world—the cruel and inescapable sorrow. It is finite reasoning to try to measure an eternal view. There are no explanations for even a fraction of the "whys" that can plague our lives. I don't know why some starve and others feast. Some die; some live. But I do believe that in the final sum of things, God is fair.

Corrie ten Boon, a survivor of a Jewish concentration camp, recalls how her father gave her a way to deal with questions that didn't have immediate answers:

> He turned to look at me, as he always did when answering a question, but to my surprise he said nothing. At last he stood up, lifted his traveling case from the rack over our heads, and set it on the floor.
>
> "Will you carry it off the train, Corrie?" he said.
>
> I stood up and tugged at it. It was crammed with the watches and spare parts he had purchased that morning.
>
> "It's too heavy," I said.
>
> "Yes," he said. "And it would be a pretty poor father who would ask his little girl to carry such a load. It's the same way, Corrie, with knowledge. Some knowledge is too heavy for children. When you are older and stronger you can bear it. For now you must trust me to carry it for you."
>
> And I was satisfied. More than satisfied—wonderfully at peace. There were answers to this and all my hard questions—for now I was content to leave them in my father's keeping.[4]

Though the answers are not often apparent, they exist. It is not naiveté but part of our peace to place the questions in a suitcase and allow our Father in Heaven to carry it for us until the time comes for further enlightenment.

The challenge is that our histories are written like complicated poetry without explanations. Even though we may not understand the "dealings of . . . God" (1 Nephi 2:12), we can pray for softened hearts and sensitivity to quiet impressions that we belong to Heavenly Father. The beginning to testimony is always a softened heart and prayer.

Opened Heavens

Through personal revelation, the heavens are opened to each of us. Sometimes it is as though we are afraid to even speak of personal revelation, to assume that we could be worthy of such a blessing. But Elder Bruce R. McConkie states, "Now I say that we are entitled to revelation. I say that every member of the Church, independent and irrespective of any position that he may hold, is entitled to get revelation from the Holy Ghost; he is entitled to entertain angels; he is entitled to view the visions of eternity; and if we would like to go the full measure, he is entitled to see God the same way that any prophet in literal and actual reality has seen the face of Deity."

Elder McConkie also gave a simple formula for receiving personal revelation:

1. Search the scriptures
2. Keep the commandments
3. Ask in faith.[5]

One of the most beautiful prayers I have ever heard was when kneeling with a friend and two missionaries who were teaching her. She began her prayer with difficulty, not because she lacked faith but because she was in awe that she could speak to Heavenly Father. She spoke reverently, "Heavenly Father."

The Spirit seemed to pour down upon us as a sign that Heavenly Father was listening. My friend humbly continued her prayer, holding a little instruction card the elders had given her. She thanked her Divine Maker for her family, her friends, and the missionaries, asking for blessings and concluding in the name of Jesus Christ. I was honored and blessed to be kneeling in that holy sanctuary around her kitchen table. Within my heart burned a deep conviction of the truthfulness of the gospel of Jesus Christ.

The Bible Dictionary teaches that prayer is a form of work. It requires energy and self-control. It is imperative that we discover that there are blessings with our name on them, waiting for our request.

Praying may seem strange because it will vibrate strings of the heart that may have been quiet for many years. Refuse to squeeze those strings with doubts, but allow hope to make room for the rich and wonderful melody that will flow from faith. Don't set up stipulations on how God needs to answer a prayer; simply allow Him to be to in charge.

Our development will continue as we read the holy scriptures and earnestly search for answers in our lives. Seeking is of no use unless we live out our day in such a way that we can receive answers to prayer. We must determine to judge between evil and good, and then act in line with our conscience.

Through the realm of spirituality will come the realization that we are not on our own. With patience, we will be able to hear Him calling from a distant home, assuring us that we are loved and known.

Our Inherited Glory

Because we are His children, our Heavenly Father has given us a portion of His glory. Because of this glory, we are important even in our smallness. As the poet William Wordsworth said, "Our life's Star, Hath elsewhere its setting, And cometh from afar: Not in entire forgetfulness, And not in utter nakedness, But trailing clouds of glory do we come From God, who is our home."[6]

This truth will be brought to our remembrance in personal ways—dark storms, threatening waves, sunny walks, astounding miracles, and quiet assurance. The sure thing is that our Heavenly Father will give us a way to feel love, joy, and purpose. In the ocean of life, we associate with family, friends, and even nameless faces. We learn of our smallness, yet also gain the ability to rescue.

Our abilities, including the ability to keep the commandments, are strengthened as our testimony and love of Heavenly Father and Jesus Christ increase. One evening my husband and I joined with our five children for family night. We were talking about keeping the commandments. Our oldest son had just returned from a mission. His life and heart had been changed by the love and testimony gained during his mission. I will never forget his insightful remark: "We keep the commandments not because we are afraid of Heavenly Father, not just to receive blessings, but because we love Him and do not want to make Him sad." Knowing of our close relationship with Heavenly Father brings sweet solace, strength, and a desire to serve Him.

We can attempt our journey through life alone—claiming our independence. But as we claim our independence, we must also claim our stupidity and realize that without fins we are choosing a weak and lonely swim against the current. We must acknowledge that we are choosing darkness instead of light (see Helaman 13:29).

Our relationship with Heavenly Father did not start here on this little planet. Just as He, we have always existed in a realm that has been wisely hidden from our memory. With love beyond our comprehension, He looked upon our spirits and wanted us to live as He lives, with His glory. Through His godly powers, He established the laws that were necessary for our creation, growth, and salvation. We are literally His spirit daughters, and because of this we are able to gain knowledge, develop divine attributes, and receive the gift of eternal life!

Our Father's love was manifest in the birth and mission of Jesus Christ, the Only Begotten, our Redeemer, who is named Wonderful, Counsellor, the Mighty God, the Everlasting Father, the Prince of Peace (see Isaiah 9:6)! And because of Him and through Him, we are able to approach the Father of us all.

Even in our small understanding of Heavenly Father and His unbounded love, His complete intelligence, and His eternal graciousness, we are overwhelmed with awe. What if we could remember His presence? We would never have a test because we would never turn our heart or mind from reverence and worship of Him.

Oh the times I have wished to remember what it felt like to be near Him! To remember the touch of His hand or the warmth of my soul as His words entered my heart. Oh that I could remember the breathtaking rapture in the air as He passed by, or looking up into His holy, radiant face as I sat at His feet.

Even though we do not remember these things, through the Holy Ghost we can remember and assuredly know that we are His treasured daughters. Our diamond can be revealed from the waste of dullness, darkness, and doubt. Such witness is borne as we increase our yearnings to draw unto Him and to be like Him. It is a magnificent facet tenderly cut by Heaven's revelation. As we relish the eternal truth of our divine nature, we will arise and shine forth in God-given splendor.

Notes

1. Neal A. Maxwell, "The Man of Christ," *Ensign*, May 1975, 101.
2. Richard G. Scott, "The Power of a Strong Testimony," *Ensign*, Nov. 2001, 87.
3. "The Family: A Proclamation to the World," *Ensign*, Nov. 1995, 102.
4. Corrie ten Boon, *The Hiding Place* (New York: Bantam Dell, 1984), 26–27.
5. Bruce R. McConkie, "How to Get Personal Revelation," *New Era*, June 1980, 46.
6. William Wordsworth, "Ode: Intimations of Immortality from Recollections of Early Childhood," lines 60–66.

chapter 6

Muster Courage through Adversity
when cloud nine rains

During the Revolutionary War, the British paid the Indians a bounty for the scalps of men and boys or for the capture of boys whom they could mold into soldiers. One cold night in 1780, a band of three hundred Indians, led by British troops, raided farms in Vermont. The Indians pirated men and boys to sell for the bounty offered by the British.

The Hendee family had been warned, and the husband set off to warn others downstream. Hannah Hendee picked up her young daughter and ran to the woods with her seven-year-old son, Michael. The Indians caught them and took Michael. When Mrs. Hendee demanded to know what they would do with the boy, one of the Indians in English replied, "Make a soldier of him."

As the Indians dragged away the sobbing little boy, Mrs. Hendee carried her screaming daughter toward the road and hurried toward the nearest town, sixteen miles away.

> She had not gone far when she was filled with a surge of uncommon resolve, a fierce determination. She returned upriver and found the British and the Indians gathering their captives. . . .
>
> Oblivious of the danger, she demanded her little boy. Captain Horton said he could not control the Indians; it was none of his concern what they did. She threatened him: "You are their commander, and they must and will obey you. The curse will fall upon you for whatever crime they may commit, and all the innocent blood they shall here shed . . . will cry for vengeance upon your head!"

75

When her little son was brought in, she took him by the hand and refused to let go. An Indian threatened her with a cutlass and jerked her son away. She defiantly took him back and said that she would follow them every step of the way to Canada, she would never give up, they would not have her little boy!

Finally, intimidated by her determination, Captain Horton told her to take her son and leave. He could face an army of men, but not a mother driven by the strongest of emotions. . . .

During the day other little boys were brought into camp. Desperately they clung to Mrs. Hendee. With uncommon courage, she interceded for them as vigorously as she had for her own.

Finally, when the captives were assembled for the long march to Canada, (Hannah) Hendee somehow crossed the river with her daughter and nine small boys. . . . Two of them she carried across. The others waded through the water with their arms around each others' necks, clinging to her skirts. As the cold October night closed in, Mrs. Hendee huddled in the woods with the soaking-wet little brood she had rescued from certain death.[1]

Courage during adversity will enable us to not only live our dreams but to help others who are in their own captivity or distress.

Through adversity, we will experience our own "Hannah moments" while crossing a dangerous river with others clinging to our skirt. These moments are an education of courage and the opportunity to prove to ourselves who we really are, to give ourselves history—a record of existence and our response to difficult situations.

Because of our personal strength—developed in the adversity that we once wished away—we will have the ability and courage to reach the bank of safety and rest.

It is not only in swimming to the bank of the river that courage will be important, but in the rushing water, the freezing temperatures, and even the whirlpools. Such elevating lessons highlight weaknesses and present an opportunity to depend upon the Lord.

Truman Madsen explains,

> Ether 12 makes it clear that God gives men weaknesses. He does this in at least two ways.
>
> First, we are all born into a world of weakness, a fallen world of infant dependence and of opposition and contrast on every hand. We enter this

mortal world with weaknesses in our physical and genetic makeup; some we may bring individually from our pre-mortal existence. Some weaknesses are the inheritance from previous generations. The Lord may have customized—with our full consent—our particular obstacle course to those flaws and failings as well as to our strengths.

Second, out of his love for us, God is the giver and the withholder of gifts. "To every man is given a gift," but "all have not every gift" (D&C 46:11; see also Moroni 10:17). It follows that to receive one is to be denied others. For the meek, both realities lead to a realization of the loving dependence we have on God and the interdependence we share with each other. We thus begin to see ourselves with new eyes: "If men come unto me I will show unto them their weakness" (Ether 12:27). Then comes the crunch. Will we resent or repent? Will we permit his mercy and his long-suffering to have full sway in our hearts and bring us down to the dust in humility? (See Alma 42:30.)[2]

Adversity alone does not have power to transform weaknesses to strengths, nor sinner to saint. But relying on the healing power of the Atonement, which lightens burdens of all varieties, will save us from bitterness, despair, and character shrinking. We must choose to use it.

During BYU Education Week 2004, Jack Rushton spoke of the purpose for our adversity. He said, "If it doesn't make us more dependent upon the Lord, rather than on the arm of flesh, that adversity will be wasted on us."

I squirm at the thought of pain and adversity. Still, our birth did not include wings of escape. Such problems are both earth's nature and a divine design. We were born to experience failure, miss the target, come up short, and ultimately enjoy invigorating success.

My Mother's Legacy

Mother always said, "We will find a way." She was right, for although there were seven children left at home without a father, we would never be denied the necessities of life. We enjoyed the luscious pleasures of romping in pastures, cooling our feet in the creek, and the treasured companionship of siblings. Mother taught me that happiness was for everyone and, even more important, that happiness is a responsibility, not a gift. So life was hard—to an extent; why should I make such a deal of that? Wasn't there enough goodness that I could find reasons to be happy? And wouldn't it be better to share the happiness I found than to have an empty-pocket attitude?

I abhorred receiving pity from anyone. That mind-set was Mother's legacy. It felt dishonest to accept "You poor thing, Mary" because I knew that somehow our problems—our rainstorm—had showered us with blessings. They may have been disguised: the blessing of learning to sew and tailor came from the lack of money to shop at department stores. Creativity and a keen eye for a way to make do came as a result of not running to the store for every little part. Talents were learned as a result of the absolute need to know how to live. And independence and strength were honed through loneliness.

Makeup Calls

My husband, Al, and I have reared a family of sports maniacs. Sons and daughters alike could dribble a basketball before they could read. My donation to this passion was my 5'11" height. My mother always told me that someday I would be happy I was tall! One time my mother-in-law asked my eight-year-old son if he was the smartest student in his class. He straightened his shoulders and with a gleaming smile reported, "Well, I'm not the smartest, but I'm the tallest!" I call this Stosich Mentality. Under great duress, I finally let our children give up the piano bench for the team bench. They loved sports, and my husband and I loved watching our "stars" play ball.

The great amazement to all parents—usually half of them at a time—is the one-sided calls of a referee. These calls always receive wild responses from the crowd. But the game goes on, back and forth. Bad calls, good calls, and some makeup calls.

A makeup call, according to Stosich Mentality, happens when the referee makes a call that tries to make up for a disadvantage. It's a legal way to even out the score.

A great phenomenon of real life is a makeup blessing. It is when God gives us an opportunity to develop a particular talent so that we can make up for a painful shortfall. A sort of heaven-sent extra credit.

Mosiah describes the slavery of the Nephites to the Lamanites. Their adversity blesses them with humility, repentance, and complete dependence upon the Lord. Blessings are described in Mosiah 24:14–15, and 21:

> And I will also ease the burdens which are put upon your shoulders, that even you cannot feel them upon your backs, even while you are in bondage; and this will I do that ye may stand as witnesses for me hereafter, and that ye may know of a surety that I, the Lord God, do visit my people in their afflictions.

And now it came to pass that the burdens which were laid upon Alma and his brethren were made light; yea, the Lord did strengthen them that they could bear up their burdens with ease, and they did submit cheerfully and with patience to all the will of the Lord. . . .

Yea, and in the valley of Alma they poured out their thanks to God because he had been merciful unto them, and eased their burdens, and had delivered them out of bondage; for they were in bondage, and none could deliver them except it were the Lord their God.

Even though there are always blessings to even out the score, sometimes we are too bitter to enjoy such mercy. Those three scriptures from Mosiah teach us how to receive such wonderful blessings. First, we need repentance and faithfulness, then a willingness to stand as witnesses, cheerfulness, patience, gratitude, and profound acknowledgment of the Lord. Again I quote Jack Rushton: "We need not be terrorized or held hostage by our circumstances in life."

Would we rather trudge through mud than walk in fresh rain? What is to be found in a mudhole? The satisfaction of a phony martyr who claims, "Thy will be done," yet continues breathing, just to prove that joy is unreachable. Perhaps it is the evil hopelessness that pries our clinging fingertips from the edge, or it could even be the despairing belief that the whole entire world is the mudhole.

It has been said that in the end, everything is fair, but the real truth is that everything is weighted to our advantage.

This Wasn't the Forecast

Each of us will pass through storms. Each of us will live moments of grand heroism and even selfish cowardice. The universe, in all its grand eternity, knows how to build character, if we will accept the challenge—even if it seems like a hurricane. There is an overwhelming desire to stay safe in some sort of false security—which deep in our hearts is teetering on its pointed, fragile stilts as the water rises and the storm gathers. It is the storm, not the stilts, that nourishes our roots and gives us the necessities to succeed.

The clouds are heavy with lessons that ask for a decision. Whatever disappointments we may face, we are at the same time asked, "How will you define your life? Will it be by your tears? Will everything have a bitter memory, or will you define your life by all that flourishes from your bravery?"

When Becky Reeve was in her early twenties serving as a full-time missionary in South America, she suffered the tragedy of a car accident that rendered her paralyzed from the neck down. Doctors offered her no hope of ever sitting, walking, or even moving again. She was told she would be nothing more than a vegetable. Becky writes,

> Well, I don't know about you, but who wants to be a pea or a carrot in this life? And so, during those hours that I lay on the frame, I had plenty of time to think about what I wanted to do. And I thought . . . "What can I be?"
>
> Now I like to be something, and I don't care if there are any muscles moving or not. I don't like to be average. Average kind of makes me sick. You're as close to the bottom as you are to the top . . . Pea or carrot sounds average to me.
>
> Then I decided what I could be, and I'll never forget that inspiration. I said, "I know; I'll be a cripple. Now, I don't know how to be a cripple, but I'll be the greatest cripple who's ever lived." That thought brought joy to my soul, and that's what I've been working on for twenty years.[3]

Becky went on to finish college, though it took her eight years to complete her last four semesters. Today, she is a published author, the recipient of the Distinguished Service to Humanity Award and the Trudy Calabrese Gift of Service Award, and an advocate for the Sit Tall Stand Tall program in Provo, Utah, finding sponsors for quadriplegics who are in the program for rehabilitation. Forty-one years after her accident, in the fall of 2003, Becky took her first four steps since the accident. She has lived a life defined by a silver lining in her clouds.

Julia Bedke, a young college student, collided with a car while she was riding a bike. As she catapulted off the bike through the car's back window, her face was gashed by glass, then shredded by pavement. Julia returned to school long before her face returned to normal. Although there were many surgeries and much pain ahead, she ignored the stares and focused on her goals. She defined her life with gratitude and hope.

A few days ago, Julia called to inform me of her upcoming wedding to the paramedic who came to her assistance. They jestingly say, "Well, we really met by accident!"

Another friend and the mother of four finally left a marriage torn apart by infidelity and years of deceit. She and her children bore years of tight budgets and skimpy holidays. She told me of one Thanksgiving when her family didn't have enough money to even buy a turkey. Without losing faith, she prayed that they would be able to get through that disappointment. The day before Thanksgiving, she went out to her car and found that someone had filled it full of food and treats. Not only her determination but her trust in a brighter future, along with her faith in God, eased her anguish and helped her family to endure until easier, happier times.

I know women who have passed through nine months of anticipation, of growing love, only to deliver a stillborn baby. There are women who dream of marriage but spend years without a companion. There are other women who marry and spend years in an emotional prison. There are cancer survivors, depression victims, and financial victims. The stories of grief and uncommon valor are legion and bring many to a realization of their own ease and comfort. We are left in awe and gratitude—even hopeful for those who are less fortunate.

But, what of smaller storms? Is there not heroism in our simple, day-to-day choices? Aren't these decisions also defining? Don't they add up, bit by bit, to an amazing bottom line?

We are not on the earth to be princesses who complain if our hair gets wet from a once-friendly cloud. We will never be fulfilled if we expect our lives to run perfectly.

We are part of a vast sisterhood in which each woman endures a tempest. But be assured: we are capable of success. Our joy and wisdom are connected to our ability to embrace adversity, submit to its tutoring, and recognize its worth in our lives.

Let's set our sights on blessings. However small they may seem at first, gratitude will grow until it engulfs our chaos, our bitterness, and our disappointments. This realization leads us to a new definition of who we are.

What if?

There always seem to be promises of success if we survive the storm. But what if? What if we go through it all and nothing turns out? What if, after all those years, we still hurt? What if we are left alone anyway? The truth is that we did not default to the puny, tiny, or small. What if? It doesn't matter because of what we have become, and the universe knows it. The ripples where we stirred the water keep going and because of our goodness and courage, nothing will ever be the same.

We must understand the difference between our problems and ourselves. They may be dreary, awful, and temporarily foreboding, but we needn't be. We can still be full of light and love.

"What if?" can also apply to the flip side of the coin. What would happen if we did give up? What if we didn't change one thing? How many people would suffer? Would our family be different? At what depths would our self-esteem bottom out? What would happen to our mental health? Would we have more friends? Would we be wiser? Would we be any happier?

Running the Course

After having my fourth child, I decided to follow the example of neighbors who jogged every day, up and down the road. They often said, "Mary, come on out and try it. It's the greatest!"

I could not resist their enthusiasm. One day I pulled on a pair of old tennis shoes and ran my first mile. Winded and practically dead, I reached my front porch. I wondered how that feeling could ever turn into triumph. I had never seriously trained for any sport, and many lessons were in my immediate future.

As women, we wonder how pain can metabolize into anything desirable. We wonder how we can survive. Will morning ever come? Yes, it comes as we turn to our Creator. He will salve our wounds and stand us on our feet—different and deeper than we could have ever been on our own.

My goodness! I was not the coordinated type, just tall and lanky. I could barely reach down to touch my toes. But endurance was my rock-solid gift, so I kept jogging. You know how I looked. You have seen joggers like me on the road. Our feet barely leave the pavement and our tongues hang down to our knees. If you wave at us when we pass by, we can barely lift a finger to acknowledge you. Still, we think we're jogging because we're moving.

Someone watching me may have had a good laugh. My gangly arms and legs. Sweaty, stringy, wild hair. Weird early-morning outfits. Crazy to the core, I started a daily running regiment—even when there was a warm bed to stay in or housework that tugged at my jacket hem as I squeezed out the door each morning.

For each of us, there have been many doubters, mockers, and those without understanding. Those who thought they knew best and tried to offer an easier solution—something that didn't require so much work. There will always be those who try to discourage us and add weight to our burden. But miracles happened, even to a jogger. I gained strength and ease. I traipsed after those ahead of me, I looked at those who had already run many miles, and I listened to those who encouraged me in my quest for self-mastery.

If we didn't have opposition, what would we ever learn about ourselves? And about our well-meaning friends? We must add them to the opposition. There are times when help arrives and other times when we have to keep putting one foot in front of the other with no hope in sight. This doesn't mean we are failures. It means the Lord has not given up on us! It means we are important and have something to learn. All of these insights help us move forward. Still, there is no moving forward without resistance.

After several years of running alone, I met Patricia. We discovered our common interest in running, and she became my jogging partner. Every morning she drove to my house and by 5:00 a.m. we were jogging. Our hour-long run seemed short because we paced our sessions with inspiring conversations. We solved the world's problems and, well, when we did that, we didn't need sleep. Patricia was unstoppable, experienced, and a little out of control. I loved her!

We first ran in noncompetitive races, but then we heard of a half-marathon relay race. What was I to do? My intelligent-self realized the ridiculousness of entering this race, yet a tiny piece of me couldn't resist the enthusiasm of my other running friends. Even though I was the least experienced runner, I heard myself commit to the race. Imagine running a relay up to a ski resort!

In advance I went to the mountain and practiced my leg of the race. I knew what to expect and how I would feel. But on the day of the race, we changed positions and my portion turned out to be more difficult than I had anticipated. I felt as if I had been running for hours! It was much steeper than what I had practiced, and I began to think how foolish I was for even entering the race in the first place! My lungs burned, my legs knotted, and the only thing that kept me going was knowing that others were waiting for me and I could never disappoint them. I would rather have died. Their support helped me feel past my exhaustion.

See the climb as an opportunity and responsibility. It is easier to do something difficult when we know it will matter to someone. This is part of embracing life. These opportunities are what lead to our coronation! It is a way to share our life with untold others—of whom we may be completely unaware. There is always someone who will treasure our example, be strengthened by our faith, and rise up to call us blessed!

Then, directly in front of me, from around the bend, came one of my running friends—fresh as a daisy! She was waiting for me so she could complete the last leg of the relay. She came to cheer me on, to run the last minutes with me, and I gratefully listened to every word of her encouragement. "Keep going, Mary! You are closer than you know! You can do it!"

In a world that doubts, I offer hope and encouragement. In a world that calls me weak and unable, I must adopt a new attitude of powerful positivity. In a world that sees me as small and fragmented, I can still have a clear view of my profound influence. Though others have told me to forget it and onlookers will mock and yell, "It's not worth it!" I quietly whisper the truth: "I can. I must. I will."

To the surprise of everyone, our team won a huge three-foot trophy! First place in our age group! When my husband arrived to pick us up, he asked, "Whose trophy is that?" He couldn't believe we had won it—that is until I admitted to him that we were the only women's relay team in our age group!

We cheered for ourselves because, who else would? That is one of the biggest lessons I learned from running—I had to pretty much cheer for myself. I alone knew where I was coming from. I alone knew the price and the reward. My reward was more than a trophy. It included the day I ran along the beach with my daughter on her first visit to the ocean. It included running in a Narnia-esque snowstorm while laughing out loud. I would never trade one early-morning silver moon or pink sunrise for extra sleep or a cleaner house. I had my share of scraped knees and hands, barking dogs, and honking cars—but I wouldn't have traded it for anything!

Is life hard? Of course! Are there excruciating and disappointing events? Definitely! In fact, I am not suggesting we deny sadness, regret, or anguish. Remember the emotions on the road to coronation? It's okay to wallow in pity for a while. We can feel the sadness. We might want to sit in the middle of the floor with a roll of toilet paper and cry our eyes out. Our sobbing may come up from the depths of our soul, with wrenching hindsight. I say we should make it worth our while. We can ruin our makeup, cry out loud, and get our eyes bloodshot. But the ultimate goal is to put an end to such suffering. Pain is only part of the story. Many times the true tip-top of the mountain is found deep in the valley of our new heart. We must stop fighting against joy and simply allow ourselves to feel gratification for what we have experienced.

Each of us has a course to run, complete with those who think we are crazy, those who discourage us or diminish our worth, and those who simply don't understand. Reach for and accept the responsibility to be happy. The world is full of miracles because God wants us to meet our challenges.

As we take upon us the yoke of Jesus Christ and receive His help and love, we are able to bear our burdens, no matter their intensity. The sorrows and disappointments of our life will be the perfect pressure that takes part in the creation of our diamond. Endurance of such experiences will not end in disappointment, but in the joy of an exquisitely brilliant facet.

✳

Ashamed of all the ways that I had failed,
Ashamed that I had not won the race,
Broken,
Sore, and
Weeping,

I fell across the finish line into
His saving arms.

No chastisement for my pace!
Every pain justified in His eyes!
Grief soothed into understanding!
Knowledge enlightened fear!

And my shortcomings?
Stroked away with
His holy,
Wounded hands!

The truth that
My race had made all the difference
Raised me up.

I stood before Him, beautiful and straight;
Somehow, with
Miraculous blessings of eternity,
A winner of the race!

     —*Mary Anderson Stosich*

Notes

1. Evelyn Wood Lovejoy, *History of Royalton, Vermont,* quoted in Boyd K. Packer, *Let Not Your Heart Be Troubled* (Salt Lake City: Bookcraft), 58–60.
2. Truman G. Madsen, "I Have a Question," *Ensign,* Feb. 1985, 49.
3. Maren Mouritsen, ed., *For Such a Time as This* (Provo, UT: Brigham Young University Publications, 1982), 106.

chapter 7

Leave Your Signature
joyful creating

*T*he summer bouquet, brilliant and loud, was fresh and unique. Strange that it could just sit there while proclaiming the excellence of God! It was the eye-catcher that drew praise and conversation from many who entered the room.

I was fourteen years old when Mother unselfishly gifted me the weekly task of arranging cut blooms of the season in a vase for the mantel. However, I was not allowed to do this without first receiving instruction on focal point, line, color, variety of specimen, and size—and especially how every bouquet was meant to say something about the artist. To make each bouquet an original, Mother taught me to include wild grasses, tree leaves, and even vegetable plants. She ingeniously taught me personal style and creativity—ingredients that became my signature.

In my family's low-budget world, there was a lot of room for creativity. Imagination ruled. Hand-me-downs looked brand new, and we mixed three partially filled paint cans to have enough paint to redecorate my bedroom. One of my favorite memories was sitting, fully clothed, in our old-fashioned tub with pedestal legs while I painted wall-paper-like flowers on the bathroom wall. We had barely enough money for matching towels. My mother praised my artistry for months, and I truly felt gifted!

We are given the desire to create from a generous Heavenly Father. His omniscience is reflected in the scriptures. His joy is manifest in, "And I God, saw everything that I had made, and, behold, all things which I had made were very good" (Moses 2:31). We were sent to an intensely interesting and

87

beautifully diverse earthly sphere. It was created for our earthly sojourn. So deep and wondrous are God's creations that we barely begin to scratch the surface, never even approaching the point of "searching of his understanding" (Isaiah 40:28).

What Money Can't Buy

Our modern world is toxic to our creativity. Our consumer society tells us if we don't have it, we should simply buy it. Our brains get piled high with the rules of décor and fashion, with no regard to our innermost cravings. In fact, we are brainwashed into believing that our cravings are in front of our noses—ready for purchase. But the satisfaction seems to bead on us like water on wax, instead of soaking through to our souls. We look for more because we remain thirsty.

There are many musty role models telling us how we must look, write, sing, read, eat, cook, play, work, and live. The "musts" build to a ceiling-high stack where there is not much room left for even a moment of self-expression. We don't even realize that there is a self that would enjoy expression.

Work on it

On top of that, we are becoming increasingly fearful of work and effort—considering it drudgery instead of an opportunity.

Growing up in a matriarchal home had special rules. One rule that topped the list for my siblings and me was, "Mother knows best, and she makes the decisions." Despite the challenges our family faced, she led with strength and confidence. Her personal philosophy in no way reached modern feminism, but she believed that we were able and had the responsibility to live productive and rewarding lives.

As much as I loved my mother, I feared her power. She was my dominant influence; it was simple—I obeyed. Thus it was not surprising when one day she announced without much ado, "It is time for you to start piano lessons." Within twenty-four hours I began a journey of patience, work, sacrifice, and even dread. To Mother's credit, it was also a journey that led to a very important part of my identity—music.

With the piano, I became the recipient of Mom's continuous monitoring of counting, naming notes, hand position, and posture. Even after taking lessons for six years and reaching the mature age of twelve, my personal desires were not considered. My daily commitment was drawn from me like a confession from a criminal, and I continued to mold my body to the piano bench.

By the time I was thirteen years old and had exhausted two piano teachers, I reached what I considered to be the top of my profession. After all, I was the accompanist for the junior high choir and the organist for our church, and I had the ability to play hymns—any hymn—with exactness and expression. I had met Mother's standard.

I remember this so well because at bedtime, my brothers would call out their favorite tunes, and I would play their selections until they fell asleep. Through this creative experience, I felt love and appreciation from my brothers.

I learned that I had a talent to give that others could enjoy. Music also gave me a niche during high school. Though I didn't have a notable singing voice, my piano talent was needed for our prestigious choir. This organization provided me with social acceptance and the feelings of being an integral part of the teenage world.

Mother finally relented and allowed me to quit lessons. Even so, the experience of creating music had helped me forge my early identity.

As latter-day women, we seem afraid of our effort—not only for ourselves, but also for our children. If they complain, we are often inclined to cave in and let them have their way. We allow them to take the path of ease and least resistance, maybe because it will also be *our* way of least resistance! We need to understand that work often accompanies creativity. As we create beauty, we also create a work ethic. Without work, a project becomes a stack of reminders of what we wasted and what we will never finish. Instead of an increase in self-esteem and a new skill, we are left with frustration and regret for even beginning!

Just for Fun

There is another dimension of creativity that is simply for fun. These less-involved diversions from monotony can appease our desires to whip up something new in our corner of the world. We plant a pot of flowers, paint fresh color in a room, tie a scarf in a new way, write a short note, or nurture any other idea that renews brain cells. Although we may not call these ideas earth shaking, they refresh us like an oasis when we suffer dehydration from a dry and barren journey. Enjoyable creativity will be different for each of us according to our personal wishes.

The Three Necessities of Creativity

Three ingredients are necessary for us to develop our creativity, whether we are pursuing a long-term goal or simply taking a break.

1. *Giving Ourselves Time*

One late afternoon I opened the fridge, leaned on the door, and waited for inspiration. This was not unusual. It was my five-o'clock trance, when I chanted my mantra: "What should I fix for dinner? What should I fix for dinner? What should I fix for dinner?" My quandary wasn't too different from a teenager in the same pose whining, "What's there to eat? What's there to eat?"

I telephoned a friend who, from my perspective, was a kitchen extremist. Linda never baked just one pie—it was usually as many as a dozen. For example, every year she unloaded a pastry parade of pies for every teacher, aid, secretary, and custodian at our elementary school. Each pie was billed as a favorite. No big deal. At least that is what she claimed.

Now, standing in front of my refrigerator, all I wanted was a dinner idea—tasty and quick and enough for seven people! Linda suggested several culinary delights, but I lacked the ingredients for any of them. Several times I replied, "Well, that one won't work. I don't have all the makings." Finally in exasperation my friend gave me an "Aha!" moment: "Mary, you can't fix a meal if you don't have anything in your fridge!"

It is the same with our creativity. We can't have any fun or do anything special if we don't have the right ingredients, including time.

Sometimes our efforts require breaking a rule or habit. If we are in a race, there is no time to tie a bow on a package. Creativity demands that we look at our relentless shoulds and musts, then consider the poetry of life. Such poetry is our satisfaction, pleasure, and indulgence in the beauty of the world around us. We somehow bring these two competing worlds together to function in our lives. We must save our precious life from meaninglessness. Sometimes it is worth it to just let a task go unfinished for the sake of renewal.

Nothing can destroy my house faster than a sewing project. Play-Doh in the carpet, milkshakes still dripping from the ceiling, paints and brushes smeared across the dining table, and a DVD playing for the third time without anyone watching it. Sewing projects were relief from mundane routine, and then surprisingly the mundane routine was a relief from the sewing project. I can't say that trying to be creative was all fun and games, but it certainly made life interesting.

I couldn't often immerse myself behind my sewing machine and expect a happy family. Still, I decided I would do it sometimes and do it without feeling guilty that everything didn't run smoothly.

Thank goodness creativity does not always demand the time it takes to complete a sewing project. We can begin to look for ideas that interest us. One mother told me that she began writing on scraps of paper and tossing them in a box. Years later her efforts are a treasure chest of memories and clever writing that she is presently crafting into a book.

It is not necessary to redo our entire life in order to add beauty. It can be as simple as folding napkins, dancing to music, or trying a new color of lipstick. To create we must simply be conscious of the moment. Through a portion of his poem, Wilfred A. Peterson expresses what I think is a true artist's prayer:

Teach me the art
Of taking minute vacations
Of slowing down
To look at a flower;
To chat with an old friend
Or make a new one;
To pat a stray dog;
To watch a spider build a web;
To smile at a child;
Or to read a few lines from a good book.
Remind me each day
That the race is not always to the swift;
That there is more to life
Than increasing its speed.
Let me look upward
Into the branches of the towering oak
And know that it grew great and strong
Because it grew slowly and well.

Our busyness may seem useful and needed, but upon closer examination, we may learn that a portion of it is truly a hindrance. Change may feel like emotional surgery as we cut out something we thought we could not live without. But our pain is relieved as we begin to enjoy the beauty and fun that comes from developing our creative side.

2. Losing the need to be right or to be the best.

In a college writing course, I had the nerve to beg my professor to accept some of my poetry for an assignment. In hindsight, I was a glutton for punishment. My professor finally agreed. He showed my work to a colleague, and then I was kindly but boldly told, "You really need to read some 'good' poetry."

Was my writing the best? Was it praiseworthy? Obviously not to them. Even so, my poetry is not buried because it didn't pass. I continue to write because I love the creative moment. It gives me self-expression and a challenge.

We all too often tie our hands with self-imposed comparison: "I'm not good enough. Why am I wasting my time like this? No one else will like this." These self-defeating pronouncements make us feel useless, lifeless, and boring.

How wonderful it would be if we could free ourselves from worrying about what others think, if we could have a sense of humor and laugh at our mistakes! Of course, some of our projects will fall apart, but we aren't obligated to waste our time caring about that. Maybe we will even be inspired on a new way to proceed! We can love what we do because it's fun to do it and because the process is and always will be imperfect. Finally, we must remember that there is no nobility in being superior to another person. True nobility is being superior to our past self.

3. Finishing

One thing that can discourage us from ever attempting another creative project is leaving things undone. We need the resolve to see things to the end. Refraining from dabbling in several things will provide the time to finish one. The charactered side of us begs for completion because it validates the entirety of our effort. After all, who will read the thank-you note we didn't send?

This doesn't mean that we can't change our mind and decide partway through that we despise the process. Even that is finishing. We can stop the lessons or we can haul something out to the trash, but if canceling lessons or taking trips to the trash is more common than crossing the finish line, we might benefit from a new attitude of patience.

Becoming a finisher includes the dirty work at the end, where we clean up the mess, put things away, and restore order. For me, this meant the Play-Doh, the ice cream on the ceiling, the paintbrushes in the middle of the kitchen floor, and my own sewing mess!

Acknowledgment and Preservation

We can use our creativity to underscore the importance of our families and draw attention to meaningful experiences.

Our second son had an old SUV named "Wilda Beast." It was his pride and joy. It had to be sanded, painted, overhauled, and fed enormous amounts of gas and oil. Even so, that old SUV was treasured more than a new sports car.

"Mom, in the morning I am going to take you for a ride." Ted grinned.

The next morning I put on my jacket and boots, and I acted as tough as I could when I swung open the front door of his truck. I watched his excited fingers put the key in the ignition. He revved the engine, and we were off to the hills.

"This is where I like to go four-wheelin', Mom."

We went straight up and straight down. Again and again. I bumped my head on the roof. I screamed. I laughed. I ignored my plight and treasured my flight!

Finally, at the bottom of a hill, we stopped. I gasped! There—up the hillside—was a patch of ornate autumn weeds.

"Ted, Look! There are millions of them! They're gorgeous! Look at the pods and the color!" I went on and on.

"Okay, Mom."

We got out of the truck, hiked up, and broke off armfuls of weeds. We carefully placed them in the back of his truck, and it was the perfect ending to a beautiful autumn morning.

Every time I see the wreath I made from those weeds, I remember four-wheelin' with Ted. It commemorates a memorable experience with a son who is now grown and gone. The wreath was my signature of a precious moment.

We would be wise to look around for the chances to use our creative side. Traditions and celebrations become splendid and memorable when we are willing to follow up with creative, personal touches.

My husband and I enjoyed one sweet summer when one of our daughters and her friend spent the semester break with us. During this time, our daughter celebrated her birthday. Her friend wanted to make the day extra special.

I suggested that she go out into the flower garden and pick flowers for a birthday bouquet. She had never arranged flowers, let alone picked them. After she finished with this task, I sent her to the craft store to buy organdy ribbon for a bow. With a little help, she created a stunning centerpiece. She was speechless with her accomplishment, awed by the beauty of the partnership between herself and God's creation. She was full of joy and could hardly wait until her gift was presented.

Gratifying experiences come through using our creativity to bless another. No matter the level of skill, every art form passes from the giver's heart to the receiver's soul. The reward goes both ways.

We will find opportunities throughout our day when we can proudly sign our name to a creative project. Maybe it will be as complicated as an oil painting or as simple as setting the table. Magic happens as we give ourselves time to enjoy creativity, the sense to begin such grace without comparison, and the reward of finishing.

The principle of joy in creation is exemplified by our Savior. Out of profound love for us, He created a magnificent world full of wondrous beauty. As we follow Him with our awareness, our work, and our patience, we are blessed by the pleasure and dazzle of another facet of our diamond. It is a gift to ourself and to the world—our own personal signature.

chapter 8

Turn Mountains into Molehills
the freedom of forgiveness

Imagine the challenge of rearing twelve sons! Imagine, even further, being one of those sons with eleven brothers. What if you were next to the youngest, despised because of obvious extra attention and love from your father, then further despised because you related a dream that you had about your family? Not an ordinary dream, but one that would be a potential nightmare for your brothers—a dream in which you ruled over them! Such is an account in the Old Testament.

Joseph? "Honorable" Joseph? They must bow to the little punk? He was already a disgusting favorite of Father with his new coat, and now this fantasy of his own greatness?

Big brothers usually don't take too well to a little brother trying to get the best of them. These brothers were held captive by their lack of understanding and their condemnation, anger, and envy. Their boiling hate became too much to resist, and they plotted Joseph's demise.

Instead of murdering their own brother, however, they threw Joseph into a pit—a hole perhaps no deeper than the pit of envy, anger, and lies that restrained their own hearts.

We are not told how Joseph must have agonized over such a betrayal. We are not told of a young man, brokenhearted—sold by his own kin. We are not told if he wonders if his father still thinks of him or if anyone will search for him. We are not told of his cries to God or of his search for meaning in his isolation. What we do know is that Joseph continues living, relying on faith and obedience to chart his course.

Joseph begins his Egyptian sojourn as a slave to Potiphar—an officer of Pharaoh. Successful in everything he does, Joseph gains the confidence of his master to the extent that he becomes his overseer. A crucible of experiences teaches Joseph the freedom of a clear conscience. It comes by forgiving false accusations and further betrayal, injustice, lies, and imprisonment—almost every human sore spot we can imagine.

Eventually, Joseph's faithfulness blesses him with the ability to become great so that he can deliver those in need. His prophetic insight and wisdom allow him to prepare Egypt for seven years of famine.

Now as a ruler in Egypt, Joseph is selling and distributing stored corn when he recognizes the ten men who bow before him—his brothers. What opportunity lays before him! If he had spent his years in anger, dreaming of revenge, it would now be payback time. But that sort of person is not who Joseph has become. He was once thrown into a pit, almost murdered, sold into slavery, cast into prison and forgotten, but now he lives a free man from the inside out. He lives not as a victim but as someone who has the power to control his internal destiny.

Like any other human being, Joseph still has memories, but unlike many human beings, he is not burdened by the ghosts of his past. He was once freed from death in a pit in the ground; yet now he refuses to live in any cavern that keeps him captive with anger or a desire for revenge. His choice of forgiveness makes him free to succeed, to live with meaning, and to feel compassion and love.

Finally, in what must have been an emotional scene, Joseph falls upon his brothers' necks, weeping and kissing them. Joseph then pours out the riches of Egypt upon them: lands, food, and livelihood. He comforts them by saying something like, "Look, it's okay what you did to me. I have had a great life and have done good things because God has been my guide."

Even after the death of their father, Joseph continues to respond with reassurance and generosity—always projecting a hopeful future. What a hero—a God-fearing man whose magnanimous life teaches us that forgiveness can dissipate revenge, that there is no reason for any of us to spend our life in a pit.

Like Joseph, we can choose peace. We can refuse to struggle with clenched teeth and a white-knuckled grip on righteous indignation.

It is not only atrocities that offend us; we are beset with things like small and silly idiosyncrasies, irritating habits, and thoughtless words spoken by others. These, too, require our forgiveness. In his book *Capturing Your Dreams,* Dr. Brenton Yorgason calls this "Benevolent Blindness." It is the heroic action of overlooking and forgiving as we go. We bury our weapons of retaliation, yet become heroes in our own right by saving ourselves from resentment. We are no longer easily offended.[1]

Mountains

Mountains of resentment become mountains of sorrow. They are often laden with cliffs of cutting words and compromised, dastardly deeds. If left to linger, the sediments almost always crystallize into hardened memories. These displays of unkindness and betrayal should have been forgiven and washed out to sea. Instead, their shadows fall with too much shade and darkness. The deep valley is not a refuge but a prison, and the victim is stunted by the lack of light.

The world's hearts are exposed and broken. The world's egos are offended and irritated. Even so, must we force the worst injustice of all upon ourselves—to live with exceeding resentment and sadness?

We often search for peace in the shadows of such mountains, all the while having a hint of truth that we will only find peace beyond the jagged horizon. Blind and sad, we are often inclined to continue along the bleak path of personal grudges and pain. It is as if we are hoping to one day use injustices as evidence that we were made to suffer. Our righteous indignation keeps us comfortably miserable. We are unable to take responsibility for our actions and reactions, and then we fall victim to our own self-ordained misery.

Moving Our Mountains

Why should we care about moving the mountains that loom before us? When we forgive, we embrace the freedom to enjoy our lives. We share the incredibly loving yoke of Jesus Christ (see Matthew 11:30), which is fitted personally and perfectly for each of us. It is a masterfully created yoke that enables us to walk the path of love and dignity. Offenses become molehills—little bumps of dirt that can be kicked aside, ignored, and ultimately forgotten.

Forgiveness is not only a gift we give to someone else; it is our own oxygen. We breathe it in, and our bad moods melt away. We breathe again, and we are more understanding. We breathe yet again, and we are not so easily offended. Each breath revives our cells with compassion until every desire for retaliation is gone. We are gloriously free.

Forgiveness is not only possible; it is a commandment (D&C 64:10).

We can experience it by creating it first in our minds. The scriptures instruct us to love with our minds as well as with our hearts and souls. I performed a scripture search at lds.org that included the words *heart* and *mind*. What a connection! There were sixty-two results! For example: "And he answering said, Thou shalt love the Lord thy God with all thy heart, and with all thy soul, and with all thy strength, and with all thy mind; and thy neighbour as thyself" (Luke 10:27).

This implies that complete love uses our brain and logic as well as our heart and soul. So, to truly love we must interrupt what would naturally enter our mind! A mind will heed the instruction to search and find attributes of another. If we desire, our minds can seek for and then gain understanding. We are able to use our new logic to add meaning and understanding to our experiences.

Along with the creation in our minds, is the creation of forgiveness in our actions. There is no braver act than a kind one when we really don't feel like it. It always seems easier to wait for forgiveness until we feel better or until we allow things to die down. The problem with waiting is that sometimes the wrong thing dies down. Being unforgiving can strangle our ability to love. We must embrace the gift of forgiveness at once. After all else, this mind-set will soften our hearts. That will make all the difference!

We then become a Latter-day Saint woman who is able to do as expressed by Elder Robert S. Wood. He gave us timely and timeless counsel in his general conference address in April of 2006: "This is not a militant church to which we belong. This is a church that holds out peace to the world. It is not our duty to go into the world and find fault with others, neither to criticize men because they do not understand. But it is our privilege, in kindness and love, to go among them and divide with them the truth that the Lord has revealed in this latter day."[2]

Forgiveness in Families

As Joseph's story of old illustrates, a family is certainly the proving ground for forgiveness. Family life seems to be unparalleled as a crucible that shapes our lives. A crucible can be defined as a severe test, and a family provides each of us with the opportunity to test our character—especially in terms of our willingness to forgive.

The people we know most intimately are precisely those who can bring us the most frustration and pain. As someone once said, "Families are the best of times and the worst of times. That is because we are so up-close and personal with those included within the wall of our homes."

We expect more from them because we love them and trust in their love. We are more vulnerable because we live side by side and know the tender parts of their psyche that are easy to injure. We learn jealousy or joy, service or selfishness, apathy or empathy. Living as a family blesses us with countless opportunities to forgive and forget or to begrudge and withhold love.

We show our love to God by showing compassion—serving our parents, brothers, and sisters, and forgiving them. We strengthen our spirituality through humbling experiences that require our efforts in making molehills out of mountains.

❋

One of my sisters related to me the following spiritual experience of forgiveness:

> Even though we are not Jewish, we had heard of a Jewish custom that every seven years denoted a time to forgive all the wrongs done to you and the debts owed to you. My husband and I discussed this and decided we would benefit from this practice.
>
> We gathered our four adult children and their spouses in our home and explained this Jewish custom. Then with great emotion, we forgave them for the pain they caused us, including in their teen years. We forgave them their financial debts. We then turned the tables. We asked their forgiveness for the mistakes we had made as their parents—anything that had brought them pain or grief. We then expressed our love, and the room fell silent.
>
> Our children wept with relief. Some even laughed when they asked us to relate what pain they had possibly caused that should be forgiven. In unison our hearts were filled with gratitude and love. It was one of the most spiritual moments of our lives, and that sweetness has lasted years later, to this very day.

Freedom's Pathway

Sometimes we are able to enjoy the benefits of the journey to forgiving and then somehow take a wrong turn and end up at our same starting point. It only takes a little twist to the left—remembering our right to be angry instead of the need to be forgiving. Residual anger and resentment may continue their pull.

Keeping on course requires corrections along the way. When we feel the pull to veer off course, we can correct ourselves by giving up any of these destructive habits:

- The need to always be right
- An insatiable desire to have our way
- Being judgmental and critical
- Reserving pain at a convenient distance for emergency ammunition

Our Savior's gift to us is mental and emotional freedom and peace. Through the Atonement, our lives change because Christ's power can fill us with His emotions. In Mosiah 26:23 we read, "For it is I that taketh upon me the sins of the world; for it is I that hath created them; and it is I that granteth unto him that believeth unto the end a place at my right hand."

Because Christ takes upon Him the sins of each of us—even those who cause pain—we could reason that instead of looking at the person who hurt us, we could look at Christ. When we realize that He has taken those sins upon Himself, being asked to forgive takes on a new meaning. Can I forgive Christ? This is a compelling question for which there is only one sensible answer. Through His powerful deliverance, as we give our will to His all-understanding love, we are spared further suffering—spiritually and emotionally. That is the fairness of the Atonement. It rescues not only the offender, but also the offended.

What of Our Inner Self?

Many times our spirituality is hampered by our refusal to repent and then forgive ourselves. We stop praying to our Heavenly Father because we think that in order to receive His blessings and love we must be without fault. Guilt for things we have done wrong is our cry to begin to repent. Using Enos from the Book of Mormon as an example, Elder Spencer W. Kimball teaches,

> When he found himself far out of hearing, deep in the forest where he was alone with himself, he began to convict himself of his sins. . . . he had convinced himself that he was in desperate straits, he began to put his mind in order. ". . . I kneeled down before my Maker," he said, "and I cried unto him in mighty prayer and supplication for mine own soul . . ."
>
> The sincerity of his change of heart is manifested in his extended efforts . . . (Enos 3–4.)
>
> When this spirit is in the transgressor and he has placed himself at the mercy of the Lord, he begins to receive the relief which will eventually develop into total repentance.[3]

Forgiving ourselves brings us closer to self-improvement because it enhances our relationship with God. Carrying the burdens of past mistakes bends our heads downward. We are unable to see the streaming rays of light breaking through the clouds. Our unforgiving self takes great pleasure in contrived punishment and endlessly living in the past. It is as though by feeling the pain one more time, we could change what happened. Is this self-exhaustion a sadistic way of being important?

Let us find importance in forgiveness. Let us sing loyalty and praises to our Savior by believing Him and enjoying His promise of forgiveness.

Weekly, as we partake of the sacrament, we covenant to take the name of Jesus Christ upon us. As we take His name, or become His child, we promise to keep His commandments and stand as a witness. These commandments include forgiving others, repenting of our mistakes, and forgiving ourselves. No matter what offenses come our way, we still must stand as a child of Jesus Christ—one who keeps covenants. Then we are blessed with the constant companionship of the Holy Ghost. It is this process that gives us a testimony and enables us to witness for His name at all times, in all things, and in all places.

A magnanimous life is not created overnight. Still, the process of becoming such a person is sweet. Self-pity can't compare to freedom. Our vision is enhanced because our ominous mountains have vanished. We offer mercy and, miraculously, we are given mercy. Our resolutions create incredible love, patience, and respect for others; and in turn they build self-respect. We find ourselves enjoying our life and our fellow beings.

From the radiating beauty of our diamond, we learn there is no other way except through the Atonement of Jesus Christ that we are able to shine with inspired understanding. Making molehills out of mountains is a facet of great power. It is the power that forgiveness and repentance pour upon us to bear all things and believe all things. It is the power of love in action. It is power of divine origin that is bestowed with infinite graciousness.

Notes

1. Brenton Yorgason, *Capturing Your Dreams* (Provo, UT: Lighthouse Publishers, 2003).
2. Robert S. Wood, "Instruments of the Lord's Peace," *Ensign*, May 2006, 95.
3. Spencer W. Kimball, *Miracle of Forgiveness* (Salt Lake City: Bookcraft, 1969), 157.

chapter 9

Put All Your Eggs in One Basket
risking intimacy

Chris was a handsome young man in his mid-twenties. I was a sort of substitute mother to him, and he sat at my kitchen counter, contemplating marriage to the young lady he had fallen in love with.

"How can I know for sure?"

He wanted me to answer the question of the ages. Could I look in my crystal ball?

Wouldn't we all like the answer to Chris's question? It would fix not only the dilemma of who to marry, but many others. It would be like reading the last chapter of the book first. We would know the end of every story at the very beginning, but just like a book, a predestined life would not be worth living.

Perhaps Chris was asking, "What is my risk?" There is no simple answer to his deep question, but I could tell Chris and many others what they *can* know:

- No matter how we feel when we make the decision, there will surely be a time when we will question if it was right.
- After our decision is made, we will need to work and fight to defend it.
- The outcome will be the sum of our courage and love.

The Problem Is Not the Basket

We fool ourselves into thinking that it's the basket that has us worried. There are different baskets for different risks, such as family, friendship, and marriage. We carefully place our fragile eggs in the bottom, then stand still for fear they'll fall through. Then we wonder what is wrong with our decision. What happened here? I thought long and hard. My feelings were so clear. But really, it's not the basket at all. It's because someone didn't put an arm through the handle and start walking.

When we finally understand that we flourish in risks, we can use them as a way to be happy, not as a way to stifle our dreams. We will realize that putting our eggs in the basket never meant they were free from danger; it simply meant that we were ready to proceed.

Realizing that our opportunity to really know someone and love them is a unique talent, let us consider the words of Matthew:

> For the kingdom of heaven is as a man travelling into a far country, who called his own servants, and delivered unto them his goods.
>
> And unto one he gave five talents, to another two, and to another one; to every man according to his several ability; and straightway took his journey.
>
> Then he that had received the five talents went and traded with the same, and made them other five talents.
>
> And likewise he that had received two, he also gained other two.
>
> But he that had received one went and digged in the earth, and hid his lord's money.
>
> After a long time the lord of those servants cometh, and reckoneth with them.
>
> And so he that had received five talents came and brought other five talents, saying, Lord, thou deliveredst unto me five talents; behold, I have gained beside them five talents more.
>
> His lord said unto him, Well done, thou good and faithful servant: thou hast been faithful over a few things, I will make thee ruler over many things: enter thou into the joy of thy lord.
>
> He also that had received two talents came and said, Lord, thou deliveredst unto me two talents: behold, I have gained two other talents beside them.
>
> His lord said unto him, Well done, good and faithful servant; thou hast been faithful over a few things, I will make thee ruler over many things: enter thou into the joy of thy lord.
>
> Then he which had received the one talent came and said, Lord, I knew thee that thou art an hard man, reaping where thou hast not sown, and gathering where thou has not strawed:
>
> And I was afraid, and went and hid thy talent in the earth: lo, there thou hast that is thine.

His lord answered and said unto him, Thou wicked and slothful servant, thou knewest that I reap where I sowed not, and gather where I have not strawed:

Thou oughtest therefore to have put my money to the exchangers, and then at my coming I should have received mine own with usury.

Take therefore the talent from him, and give it unto him which hath ten talents.

For unto every one that hath shall be given, and he shall have abundance: but from him that hath not shall be taken away even that which he hath.

And cast ye the unprofitable servant into outer darkness: there shall be weeping and gnashing of teeth. (Matthew 25:14–30)

It won't matter what you wish or feel if you don't step forward. Risking intimacy is not about feeling. It is never about a buckled-down fact that we are safe. It is about doing something anyway. The dream that there is no danger is just that—a dream. We live in a world where dreams only come true after risk, courage, and commitment.

Cautious Hearts

In one way or another, each of our hearts has been injured. We have personal stories of loss and disappointment that readily reappear whenever we need a reason to give up. We have each been taught, by painful injury, to be cautious. Caution is wise. It can prevent overdrafts at the bank, poor grades in school, speeding tickets, and even divorce. But when we are cautioned into debilitating avoidance from our very reasons for existence and happiness, we also become injurious to others and begin a new cycle of pain.

I began my marriage with a handicapped heart. It had been torn when my father died and had healed with a few impeding scars. It was a heart within a stiff, heavy glove. The beating was there, the rhythm was perfect, but it couldn't quite get the job done.

My risk meant that I should pour love out to my husband without keeping score, that I could be gentle, as I deeply desired to be, without worrying that I might be rejected. It meant that I must rely on him and count on his love flowing back to me. Still, his love must be what he chose—not something in line with my expectations.

This risk meant that I would need to uncover the emptiness and allow intimacy with my husband, with God, and with other loving people.

Fear of rejection freezes into a personal rock of ice. Tears keep plopping in huge splats that freeze on contact. Over time, freezer burn ruins the soft, the dear, and the giving.

How could I risk such soul-borne intimacy? How could I risk it with another human being who was sure to make mistakes, need forgiveness, and require my lifelong understanding?

More than thirty years have passed, and I marvel that I thought I was safe in a deep rut of self-protection. How could I ever think my life would be great without a breathtaking gamble? I learned that not taking the risk was actually the greater risk. It meant giving up on everything that brings joy, then settling down in a self-made dust bowl.

I marvel that the miracle of time kindly showed me the way. A little here, a little there. Many times I simply willed trust to happen with a flat-out decision. I learned that the feeling of comfort never came when I was on the edge of the diving board.

Humanity's Risk

The risk of intimacy is not merely between husbands and wives; it is a risk of humanity. It involves receiving help, asking for advice, accepting and giving love, tolerating differences, taking another's point of view, and compromising for the good of others.

Intimate relationships set great people apart from the average. These people know how to treat others and how to self-disclose and safely receive others' disclosures. They sit on a bus and cheerfully greet their fellow travelers. They care enough to ask or to pay a generous compliment. In short, they impact a stale world with fresh air.

A family had just been relocated hundreds of miles from their home. The mother had taken her three children shopping to buy diapers and milk. But when she wrote out the check to pay for the items, the clerk could not accept it. It was a starter check with no permanent address imprinted on it.

Dismayed and overwhelmed, with no other way to pay, the mother begged the clerk to take her check, but then from a distance down the waiting line, a man—unknown to the mother—called out, "I will pay for her purchase!" Gasps and smiles of delight were the applause for the generous man. The woman next in line proclaimed, "Now you know how much God loves you!" The mother expressed to me her profound gratitude for such kindness in a difficult situation. She said, "Not only my day, but my outlook of the whole ordeal of moving changed. I really knew I would love living there."

As we feel compassion, our intimacies with others will allow God to work through us.

Half-hearted attempts at intimacy result in putting others down. Such feelings of supposed superiority recognize the dangerous threat of another's qualities. They allow a mock relationship while carefully and selfishly meting out scarce, much-deserved compliments as though they were on an endangered species list.

Do we fear the costs of intimacy? Do we just want "happy ever after" without all the years of learning, patience, sacrifice, and encouragement? Or do we delight in growing, in overcoming, and in creating intimate relationships?

Commitment to Love Is Not Foolishness

I love going to the gym, not just to exercise but to visit with some people who have become dear friends. One day I showed up later than usual, and to my surprise one of my friends was also late. We were happy to have each other's company.

I told her that I was late because my husband went out of town and I wanted to spend the morning with him before he left. I wanted to fix him breakfast and be there to tell him good-bye. Her face brightened at my excuse, and then she related to me that her neighbor dropped in while she was preparing a lunch for her husband.

"What is the matter with you?" her neighbor demanded. "Your husband can get his own food! You are being ridiculous!"

My friend told me she felt like she had broken a law serious enough to go to prison. We laughed—a little. Truthfully, we realized how fortunate we were to love and serve our men.

So what is wrong with doing things for others even if they can do them themselves? What is wrong with loving someone so much that your service will speak for your heart? Is the new rule of relationships "Do no kind thing, nor give anything of importance"? Withholding our love is not protection; it is devastating weaponry, and it kills the person we wish to love. Maybe such a maneuver could be called "death by friendly fire."

The Chopping Block

Setting ourselves up for pain and making poor choices is not putting our eggs in a basket. It is playing egg toss with a mean opponent. Intimacy requires our keenest intellect, but even so, after the best plans and thoughts, there can still be turnabouts of life that set us off in a direction we never wanted to go. Putting all our eggs in the basket may not feel too good at times. We might wonder if we merely placed them on a chopping block—ready for deviled eggs.

Giving to someone from the heart involves a portion of our inner self that will never be the same again. Perhaps a rebellious child, an untrue friend, or a deceitful spouse will deliver this sacred portion back to you mashed and mangled. Still, time will teach that there is no sorrow in giving pure love. An ensuing, inward peace will always be nicer to live with than haunting memories of withholding love.

Here are a half-dozen ideas that are intended to encourage you to put all your eggs in the basket:

1. When you start something, you have to be strong when it falls apart, and then seek for inspiration on how to put it back together.
2. Having the strength to stand alone will also give you the wisdom to stand together.
3. You can't hope for tomorrow without living today.
4. Leveling does not mean whittling another person down to your size; it is growing in understanding until you are the same height.
5. Ripples of kindness will return to us as waves of love.
6. Always choose to create joy in another's heart.

A young mother told me of her conversation with her six-year-old daughter. The girl had been bombarded with news of the 9/11 terrorist attacks. Accounting for her own personal social wound, the child looked up into her mother's eyes and with a feeling of betrayal said, "I didn't know there were real bad people in the world."

The mother wondered if her husband would be going to war and if their lives were about to dramatically change. Torn between wanting her daughter to feel safe yet not wanting to paint a deceitful picture, my friend bent down to her daughter, put her arms around her, and replied, "We must live our lives like Jesus. Then it will not matter who dies or who gets hurt. Things might not seem okay, but really they will be okay because what really matters is who we are."

Risk will always accompany the call for action. It is our personal commitment to live with integrity that places the odds in our favor and makes the risk worthwhile. We will never be free of danger. We will never be completely safe. Nor will our decisions be perfect. Even with the risk of failure, we must do our part. But as that mother told her daughter, "What really matters is who we are."

We can remind ourselves of this as we suffer from deep loss or grueling sadness. What yearning equals that of a broken heart? But despair will only deepen if we shun the opportunities for godly love. There is a brighter way! With the Holy Ghost, we can be led closer to "perfect understanding" (Alma 48:11). We can embrace the odds—weighted in our favor—and enjoy the course of life.

A stunning, luminous facet of our diamond is the blessing of intimacy. With our lifeline secured to our Savior, we need not fear rejection. As we nourish our relationships, His healing balm provides us with strength and comfort. We will become softened by empathy with hearts drawn out in compassion. Our tender words will quietly revive the withdrawn or aching heart of another. Putting all our eggs in one basket is not risk-free, but it is the only kind of living that proves rich and worthwhile.

chapter 10

Let the Outside Do Justice to the Inside
the beautiful wrapping job

I married the man of my dreams—he's 6'3". Don't roll your eyes—I'm serious. Just go back some years with me to the eighth grade. I was already 5'9" and very blessed to lack the knowledge that I would still grow two more inches. Isn't junior high bad enough without lining the girls up on one side of the gym and the boys on the other and then having them march forward to each other—a perfect pairing for the dance?

Here came my partner crossing the gym floor, one small step at a time. I thought, *He really isn't that small, is he?*

Poor boy. Surely as he sized me up, he was stricken with the same despair. But he danced with me all right, as his shorter height gave him the vantage point of staring straight at my chest. In high school I peaked at 5'11". I felt "biggie-sized" when everyone else seemed five feet tall. Even though I was thin, I began lying on my driver's license just to be more like everyone else! How much do I weigh? Really, what a futile question! I could pass a lie-detector test.

Now you can understand why I dreamed of a 6'3" man who could actually carry me over the threshold. I thought, *He doesn't need to be rich and famous, but he does have to have bigger feet than mine.*

Among other tremendous qualities, my husband was a handsome vision of masculinity. He brought out my femininity, which was a miracle for an independent, do-it-yourselfer who would never be able to cram her size eleven foot into a tiny glass slipper. It would take years before I would learn that the blisters weren't worth it.

Like most women you talk to, my body wasn't everything I had ever dreamed of. My problem was my dream. It was a version of myself from some other gene pool. There was no appreciating my physical traits that I was unfortunately stuck with. I had all the tall-girl slouch maneuvers down to perfection. I would lean on one leg and stick my other one way out—that would cut off at least three inches. I would sit on my middle vertebrate—that was worth about two inches. It was great to lean against a wall. I could lose two and a half inches from that.

Whenever she could, my mother would stick her finger in my back and firmly suggest that I stand up straight and that someday I would be glad that I was tall. But from my perspective—which was the only one that mattered to me—compared to everyone else, I looked like a freak of nature! I spent all my resources trying to imitate someone else instead of comprehending my own beauty.

Beautiful Thoughts

Feelings take life from our attitudes, and our attitudes start with thoughts. So perhaps it comes down first to thinking beautiful. Dr. Page Bailey, who has spent over twenty-three years researching and developing programs that improve recovery experience, teaches that negative thoughts deny us access to our wondrous potential. But a positive thought gives full access to action, experience, and achievement. Our thoughts are actually biologically active structures, and we have the power to guide them, invite them, and command their departure.[1]

Simply put, a negative thought is like a virus in our personal computer. It will deny us access to our hope and confuse the truth. A positive thought is a password that shoots directly into our hard drive, where we create new feelings and attitudes.

Self-disregard blinds us to our real beauty, and I do mean our real physical beauty. We can be quite convincing that we are too something. Then we set out to drive ourselves and everyone around us crazy while we are fixated on obtaining an airbrushed figure or ageless skin. Our prophetic disappointment in ourselves sideswipes our potential. It changes future prospects because it changes our self-evaluation, and our brains work with fervor to make our thoughts a reality.

Self-appreciation is beautifying. It enhances each of our natural assets. Such an attitude is seen in our walk and heard in our speech. Our own beliefs affect the way others see us because the way we talk about ourselves influences their perception of us. I'm not suggesting that we boast, but we should give ourselves a huge break! We should not draw someone's attention to our physical faults. Our self-putdowns are a burden to our spouses and friends. They create an obstacle and the wrong point of focus. Being good to ourselves is also being good to others.

The biology of happiness and self-love creates a flow in our system that directs us toward success. Chemicals are secreted through our body according to our mood. Think of that! Our biochemical condition responds to our emotions. The first step to real beauty is in our thought processes. Our appearance and demeanor wait for the command.

Many people have told me that they can't see their own beauty and talents. They are convinced they are somehow less than amazing—as though their Omnipotent Creator made a mistake. They refuse to acknowledge His divine hand in their physical body and attributes. They give the latest fashion designer more credence and honor than they do their loving Heavenly Father, who made them with eternal purpose.

Susan Tanner, our Young Women general president, explains, "I am troubled by the practice of extreme makeovers. Happiness comes from accepting the bodies we have been given as divine gifts and enhancing our natural attributes, not from remaking our bodies after the image of the world. The Lord wants us to be made over—but in His image, not in the image of the world, by receiving His image in our countenances (see Alma 5:14, 19)."[2]

If our struggle is in our attitude and we can't seem to shake it, maybe we are not lining up our actions with what is inside. Just as the batteries of a flashlight must be lined up correctly in order to produce light, our exterior must be lined up with new thoughts. If our effort is to change our attitude, then, right along with that, we must change our actions.

What are some new habits we can acquire? What are some changes in our appearance or actions that would obviously testify that we treasure the gift of our physical body?

Make a promise to stop putting yourself down. Allow yourself to believe in your singular potential.

To Care for a Temple

Our bodies allow us eternal progression. Through the blessing of a physical body, we are submitted to the tests of mortality. We "allow the spirit to exalt itself to a nobler condition."[3] How we treat our bodies, what we do to them, and how we love them will actually affect us throughout eternity! We are told in 1 Corinthians 3:16–17, "Know ye not that ye are the temple of God, and that the Spirit of God dwelleth in you? If any man defile the temple of God, him shall God destroy; for the temple of God is holy, which temple ye are."

Have you ever truly pondered that holy temples house our spirits? What about the truth that our bodies are not even our own, that they are bought with a price by God (see 1 Corinthians 6:19–20)? How do we really care and love such a precious blessing? What is it really worth to us? Our bold dedication to protecting and caring for our physical bodies is indeed bridling our passions (see Alma 38:12).

It would be a rare treat to be guaranteed a free hour of the day to do whatever we wished without interruptions. More than likely, such a sweepstakes offer is just not going to show up in our mailbox. It is our responsibility to devote the time we need for our self-improvement. We can stake out the time and do it without feeling guilty! When we care for ourselves, we can also give the best care to others. This also helps us lose envy because we have a chance for our personal improvement.

Fabulous excuses will suddenly pop into our minds—all the reasons we can't or it's hard: "I can't leave my family at that time of day," "I can't spend the money," "I don't know how," and on and on. There is an answer to every one of them. Be creative! Look past average answers. Get around the stumbling blocks. That's why we have brains—we must figure it out!

There are times when we jump into deep water, and during the initial struggle, think that we will likely drown. There is no reason to panic. Simply hold on to the side and take some time to learn the strokes. One woman explained, "I knew I needed to get a gym membership, but I couldn't do everything everyone told me to do, so I did nothing. Consequently, I was never physically able to do what I wanted to do."

There is always a sacred starting point. It might seem embarrassingly simple, but it is sacred because it is humbling. It requires that we submit to something a little over our heads and feel a little threatened. Oh yes, we have been at such a starting point again and again, but we have no need to apologize. After all, we are real, not perfect. We are living and learning, not finished.

Doing Justice

I knocked on the door and the woman greeted me with a warm smile. Inside, a festive room decorated with children's artwork exuded cheer and tradition, and a small tree stood in the corner. The skirt of the tree was completely covered with gifts. My greatest surprise was the unique beauty of each gift's wrapping. It was thoughtful and planned—not just printed paper, carelessly taped. Each gift could have been a framed specimen of art, for no two were alike. Ribbons were wound and tied with care. Multiple bows were placed carefully on every package. Glitter and colorful ink decorated handwritten nametags that dangled like fancy earrings and announced the lucky owner of each package.

When I complimented my friend on her exquisite gift-wrapping, she explained, "Well, I have worked hard on the gift inside, and I want the outside to do justice to the inside." What a wonderful philosophy of why we should care about looking our best, how we talk, our manners, and our social skills. Our personal presentation should do justice to the good that lies within us.

On one occasion, I attended a business meeting held in a casual setting. Most of us there met each other for the first time, making first impressions acutely important since we would be working together to form a business plan.

One woman was dressed in sloppy, casual clothes as if she was ready for housework. She wore no makeup, and her hair hung down as if she had spent her morning in a war zone. It was difficult overcoming my first impressions in order to consider her ideas.

After the meeting, during some small talk, this woman said, "Well, I just refuse to get all dressed up anymore for meetings like this. I can look good if I need to, but if people just can't see through the outside, then I really don't care about working with them."

This woman's problem was that her attitude was also her camouflage. Beauty incognito! Others cannot be expected to sort through and decipher the layers on the outside until they get to something lovely. Looking our best is not a façade. It is our responsibility to give clear impressions of who we are. It takes courage to portray our great worth because then we have gone public and must answer for the way we look!

The Struggle Between Beauty and Sensuality

If we pick up any magazine we can see the falsehood: beauty equals sensuality. Sensuality tempts us to present our body as though it was a gift, but, instead, the so-called gift is a trap. The tease of seduction is deceiving in its rewards. To a woman, the ability to seduce and give pleasure immediately pleases, but before too long there is truthful realization that love and respect are not the payoff, and a painful gouge remains in the heart.

Beauty is quite different. It is also soft and becoming and may also draw others to us, but instead of an enticing trap, we give careful consideration and flood others with goodness. Where sensuality and seduction often leave others with destruction and lessened capabilities, beauty is elevating.

Being sexy in the right place at the right time is fun and harmless. It can be an important gift we give to our husband. But in our world of media-glorified sex and festering sexual appetites, women must shake off the constant expectation that being sexy is the only way to be beautiful. We must learn that true beauty includes self-respect and decency.

It seems like almost every fashion ploy is anti-modesty. It is hard to describe modesty's value when hardly anyone wants to hear about it. But being modest is one of the most liberating things I have ever done. I am liberated from comparisons to other half-naked bodies. I am liberated from extreme self-concern and the worry of my own over-exposure. I feel free from the scrutiny and attentions of vain and empty people. I can look just fine—even lovely—because my expectations are my own.

Modesty also exudes kindness. It helps others feel comfortable around us and gives them a chance to see something other than some flesh falling out of our clothes.

Not long ago, the media covered the flashing news story of a teenage girl who preferred modesty! Such a preference is so unusual that it received news coverage from *Fox News*, *WorldNet Daily*, *The Today Show*, and *CBS News*! It seems that Ella Gunderson wrote to Nordstrom's executives because she was frustrated that she could find nothing to purchase that she felt comfortable wearing. This brave young lady was on the news because she was searching for modest clothing! I admire Ella for taking a not-so-popular stand. She offers all women an example of not trying to fit into someone else's glass slipper but insisting on style with principle.

Many times we don't treat ourselves with dignity or respect because we do not know our inherent worth. We think our total sum comes up short, and we try to add value with a worthless fad. Only when we realize that each one of us, in our individuality, deserves deep regard and care will we finally emulate what is really already within us.

❋

All she ever wanted was a set of diamond earrings! The woman dreamed of them. How they would sparkle! They would be the perfect pair to wear with everything! Once in a while she stopped at the jewelry store just to admire them and wish.

They would be worth it, she mused to herself, *because if I had them I would never wear anything else!*

It was simply a vain wish, because there were too many other "places to put their money." This woman knew the diamonds were never to be hers; she could only dream.

On her birthday, the woman opened a little velvet box from her husband. *How dear*, she thought, *giving me these pretty earrings. They look so much like diamonds. If only they were real!*

She thanked her husband for the gift and put the box aside while she busied herself with other tasks.

This lady only wore her birthday earrings now and then, trading off with other fun earrings: fashionable hoops, some plastic or cut-glass beads. They were pretty much all the same to her, except a time or two, when she looked twice in the mirror at the pretty sparkle of her fake diamonds. They really did look beautiful, but they held no treasured place in her heart. She secretly saved that place for "someday in the future" just in case her husband would be able to afford the real thing.

One evening as she was getting ready for bed, the woman noticed one bare ear—a birthday earring had come loose and fallen out. Not too sad, just a little disappointed, she mentioned to her husband that it was gone.

"Gone?" he questioned her. "Where?"

"Well, I have no idea. I put them on this morning, and now one's missing."

"Where have you been today? What have you done?" He continued his unusual interrogation. "Tell me! I'll look for your earring!"

"Honey, you might as well forget it. I've gardened, cooked, and cleaned. It's no use to even search." She looked at her husband's face—overly concerned and intent about her lost earring. She was sorry to have lost his gift but wished that he wouldn't fret so much over an inexpensive earring. It seemed easier and smarter to forget about the whole thing.

The woman awakened the next morning, looked over, and saw that her husband was already out of the room. She walked into the hallway and there stood the vacuum with all its dirty contents dumped and spread across a sheet of newspaper.

What was he up to? she wondered.

The morning sun had just come through the front door. "Strange that this is wide open," she remarked out loud and swung the door shut. At that instant she saw him on his knees in the flowerbed. She opened the door again and stood watching her husband as he finger-raked the garden dirt, inspecting every inch.

He looked up at her and almost said something but then looked down at his task. For a moment she stood still, paralyzed in her deep regret and realization. All this time she had not known! She had passed over the priceless gem. She had disregarded hints from its unusual sparkle, instead considering it inexpensive—almost worthless. All this time she had what she wanted, what she had dreamed of for years. But she lived in her self-created denial by never considering that her gift was invaluable and irreplaceable.

Coming back to the present, she threw her hands in the air and shrieked an alarm that resounded throughout the neighborhood. "You didn't tell me! I had no idea! My earrings are real diamonds!"

The wailing continued as her husband arose from his knees to embrace his wife. Inconsolable, she ranted over the beauty of the earrings and her ignorance. His only reply was, "Let's keep looking."

After they finished sifting through the flower bed, the couple went into the house. They had been sitting at the counter for a few moments when the husband looked across the room to a sack of potatoes slumped in a corner. He remembered their dinner the night before—mashed potatoes. Quietly, he walked over to the sack, opened it carefully, and looked in. He shuffled a couple of potatoes and stopped.

The woman watched her husband reach in and pull out his hand, pinching the small earring while he held it up, his smile ecstatic!

She kissed him a million times! She made him a thousand more promises of her love and gratitude. Wiser now than on her birthday, this grateful woman looked into the mirror and marveled at the beauty of her real diamonds. They were incredible! They sparkled as she tilted her head and brushed her hair back.

"How exquisite," she whispered in awe and relief.

The earrings instantly became as important as their beauty. She polished them with a soft cloth, and on rare occasions when she didn't wear them—for she cherished them as tokens of her husband's love—she kept them safely in their velvet box.

Only one thing had changed: the most important thing. She now knew the value of what she had.

Recently I held the hands of my frail, eighty-eight-year-old mother-in-law. She lay in her bed, exhausted from her mortal existence. Even breathing was a painful effort. Her life had fulfilled her dreams of family, work, and friends. But even after comparing these experiences with a bedridden future in a worn, sick, and frail body, she still grasped to an amazing will to live. She caused me to ponder upon the sacred nature of our physical existence.

I wondered about our desire for a physical body even before we came to this earth. It was of such intensity that we warred for the privilege of mortality, a chance to make decisions and mistakes. We could not have been weak-hearted or indecisive. We chose earth life with appetites, passions, temptations, illnesses, inabilities, and sorrows. Earth life also beckoned us with luscious laughter and love, with moments of victory, knowledge, and beauty. I imagine we were invited by the smell of spring lilacs, the glow of sunset, the soft touch of one we love, the melody of our favorite song, and, without question, the smooth taste of chocolate. All was to be relished because of the marvelous gift of a body created in the image of God! Oh what happiness and gratitude must have filled our hearts as we learned of such a gift to clothe our spirit! It is no wonder that parting from our body indeed brings us sorrow.

Caring for this gift of unfathomable worth is an honor. No matter our years or gene pool, this facet, meticulously cut, illuminates dignity, defines uniqueness, and reveals luster. It reminds us that we are in the similitude of the Only Begotten (Moses 1:6). Held up to His light, we truly do sparkle.

Notes

1. Brenton Yorgason, *401 Selected Basic Life Teachings from the Therapeutic Work of Page Bailey* (Provo, UT: Lighthouse Publishers, 1999), 28–29.
2. Susan W. Tanner, "The Sanctity of the Body," *Ensign*, Nov. 2005, 13.
3. Melvin J. Ballard, in Conference Report, Oct. 1912, 107.

The Perfect Setting
conclusion

*I*t may surprise many, but the pathway to a beautiful life is not strewn with self-serving slogans aimed at helping us focus on our own happiness. To the contrary, in our pursuit of a Christlike life, we learn that true joy comes from looking up, reaching out, and lifting others. Like a brilliant diamond to be enjoyed, our sparkle must break forth into the light of day, rather than remaining hidden within itself. It must permeate the hearts of our family, our friends, and those in need.

✳

There is a story told of Al Hafed, the fabled farmer who leaves his home and family to search his entire life for diamonds. Al Hafed dies without knowing that the most exquisite diamonds in the world—those that would crown the heads of royalty—are obscured by their rough, un-revealing exteriors and are sitting in his own backyard.

Undiscovered. Lost. Stolen. Unpolished. Wrapped in layers of disguise. It does not matter. The real truth comes forth when the Master reaches out his hand. Just as no two diamonds are alike, no two daughters of Christ exude exactly the same qualities. With perfect skill and love, He works miracles to reveal a priceless gem. We refract light into a rainbow of pure color and incredible brilliance.

The importance of life is that we honor our Savior. We have been cut into his most precious gems, each with the capacity to exude His light through our facets of divine fortune. We are each a diamond set securely in His crown with our individuality glorifying his name. In some way, each facet cut is a choice to follow Christ, a testimony of His teachings, and an invitation to all to share His happiness. It is because of Him and through His perfect light that our own diamonds reach their greatest worth. After all, He is the master diamond cutter!

If we spend our lives glistening and shedding forth Christ's light, the day will come when we are invited to see the nailprints in His hands. We will know that our joys and sorrows are in His hands, and that they alone can save us from our flaws. On that day, we will hear the Savior speak our name and claim us as His own. Through His perfect love, we will be crowned with a tiara so exquisite and so radiant that we will scarcely believe it to be our own. We will be crowned heavenly queens, and with our eternal companion we will walk gratefully into His kingdom. And all this because we allowed our potential to be identified and sculpted by the master diamond cutter, Jesus the Christ!

Our universe must then pause in reverential hush over the loveliness of the diamond of a woman's heart.

About the Author

*M*ary Anderson Stosich is quick to admit that her claim to fame is that she is married to and still madly in love with her husband, Al. After beginning their married life in Provo, Utah, they moved to Idaho, eventually ending up in South Jordan, Utah. Mary loves being back home in the valley of her birth and childhood. She loves serving in The Church of Jesus Christ of Latter-day Saints and is presently the stake Young Women president. In her dedication to strengthening families, she has written for BYU's website foreverfamilies.net, served as a volunteer Institute instructor, speaks publicly, and counsels as a life coach.

Mary says that after volunteering as a liaison between birth mothers and adoptive parents, teaching preschool, giving piano lessons, teaching troubled youth, raising five children, chasing after fifteen grandchildren, and being married for thirty-four years, it is a natural thing to write a book just to see if someone would really pay attention!

Mary returned to college and graduated from BYU with a bachelor's in marriage, family, and human development the same December as her fiftieth birthday. "But," she says, "middle age has a reason to shout for joy—experience! Most things I have learned because I got out of bed almost every morning!"